W9-CBU-321

INSTANT SKITS

USING IMPROV TO CREATE MEMORABLE MOMENTS IN MINISTRY

EDDIE JAMES AND TOMMY WOODARD **THE SKIT GUYS**

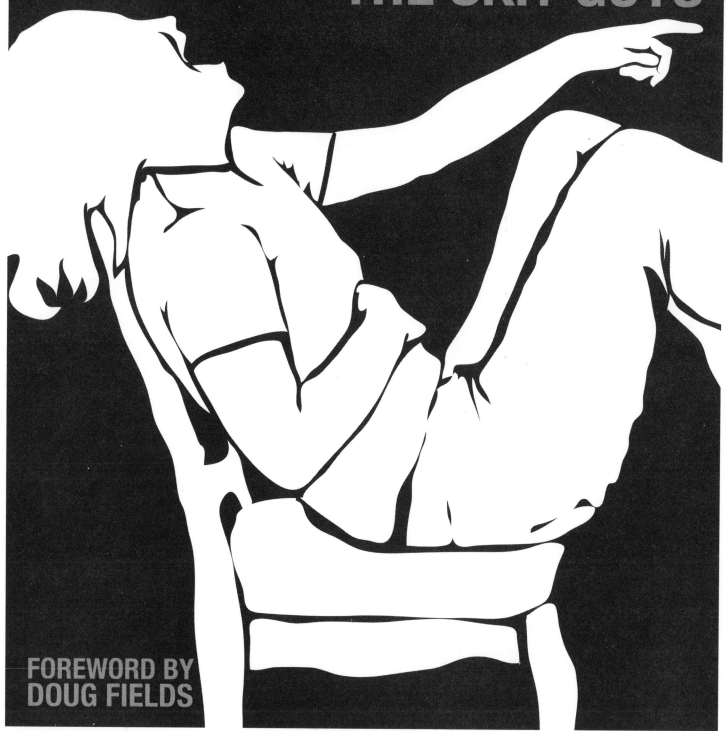

FOREWORD BY DOUG FIELDS

ZONDERVAN™

GRAND RAPIDS, MICHIGAN 49530 USA

ZONDERVAN.COM/
AUTHORTRACKER

Youth Specialties

www.youthspecialties.com

Instant Skits: Using Improv to Create Memorable Moments in Ministry
Copyright © 2005 by Eddie James and Tommy Woodard (The Skit Guys)

Youth Specialties products, 300 South Pierce Street, El Cajon, CA 92020 are published by Zondervan, 5300 Patterson Avenue SE, Grand Rapids, MI 49530.

Library of Congress Cataloging-in-Publication Data

James, Eddie, 1970-
    Instant skits : using improv to create memorable moments in ministry / by Eddie James and Tommy Woodard.
        p. cm.
    Includes index.
    ISBN-10: 0-310-26568-1 (pbk.)
    ISBN-13: 978-0-310-26568-9 (pbk.)
    1. Drama in Christian education. 2. Church group work with youth.
    3. Christian drama, American.   I. Woodard, Tommy. II. Title.
BV1534.4.J34 2005
268'.67--dc22

2005024179

Creative team Will Penner, Erika Hueneke, Mark Novelli, Brad Taylor, and Anna Hammond
Interior design by Mark Novelli, IMAGO MEDIA
Cover design by Holly Sharp
Printed in the United States of America

05 06 07 08 09 10 • 10 9 8 7 6 5 4 3 2 1

DEDICATION
Dedicated to Abby, Ainsley, and Hudson.

May you live lives full of laughter.

Special thanks to Erin MacDonald and Charissa Fishbeck.

ACKNOWLEDGEMENTS
Our wives, Stephanie and Angie, for allowing us to do what we love to do. Doug Fields, Mark Matlock, Jay Howver, Brian Cropp, Dave Rogers, Monty Priest, Gary Singleton, and all of the students who took the time to tell us some of their stories. Our lives are blessed because of you.

"Tommy and Eddie–they're not attractive, but they love Jesus and they probably actually love you. And...and...they're funny. Buy Instant Skits now!"

   - Travis Reed, founder, Highway Video

"If you want to get students involved and help locate talent within your group, Instant Skits is the book for you! The Skit Guys find out where students are, meet them there, and then teach them to use their gifts and talents through comedy and drama. This is a great resource!"

   - Ted Lowe, married life pastor, North Point Community Church, Alpharetta, Georgia

TABLE OF CONTENTS

FOREWORD

I've had the privilege of ministering and sharing life with many great people, and Tommy and Eddie are at the top of the list. There are a few reasons why I'm at the front of the line to be The Skit Guys' fan club president:

1. They love God and are totally committed to following him with all their hearts.
2. They love students and are driven by a desire to see them deepen their relationships with God.
3. They are masters of their talents and gifts and have made drama a craft.
   (A fourth reason is that they're actually quite adept at constructing Popsicle houses and making others laugh—especially me.)

If you've ever had the opportunity to see them on stage, you know all of the above is true (well, minus the Popsicle houses part).

When I need good youth ministry products, I look for resources that are easy to figure out (this is), high quality (ditto), and simple to use in any setting (my students loved it). This book hits the mark on all three qualifications.

An added bonus of this book is that it provides you and I, as youth workers, fun and easy ways to get students active and involved. There are few things more exciting in youth ministry than watching students pick up a book, figure it out, take a little ownership, and turn it into a ministry opportunity—and this resource will make the latter happen.

During my years in the youth ministry trenches, I've learned the importance of communicating truth in a variety of ways. The message stays the same, but our methods change. Skits, drama, and improv are great methods to share truth and relevance in fresh and creative ways—ways that will benefit your youth ministry setting.

Tommy and Eddie are proof that screwballs can further God's kingdom as effectively as anybody. Do you have that "one kid" who's just a little bit off the beaten path? Hand him this book, connect him with others, and you may be watching the next generation of Skit Guys.

My prayer is that this book will inspire you to get students more involved in doing ministry—and put a smile on your face.

Doug Fields

Pastor to Students—Saddleback Church

President—Simply Youth Ministry

1.0

INTRODUCTION

What is it about reality television that draws us in and keeps us glued to our TV screens? Is it the anticipation of the unknown? Is it the danger of unpredictable human behavior? Is it the knowledge that people could fall in love, a fight could break out, or somebody might have to eat a scorpion? (Yuck.) We think the appeal of reality TV can be summed up in one word: spontaneity.

The same appeal that draws millions of people to TV sets every night can be used by you to draw people to your events and keep them there, because the same spontaneity found in reality TV is also found in the art of improvisation—a situation in which actors are provided with a background, setting, and characters from which they spontaneously invent dialogue and actions. The audience provides an overall direction for the actors to go; then they take off. No one knows where they're going to go or how they're going to get there, but we all want to see how it plays out. It could be funny, or it could be serious; it could be memorable, or it could be a disaster. (Or it could be memorable, because it was a disaster.) No matter how it goes, we want to watch it happen.

At this point, you may be asking, "Why *should* I use improvs?" We're glad you asked! To help you understand why, we've compiled a list entitled—yep, you guessed it—"Why Use Improv?"

WHY USE IMPROV?

1. Using improv boosts group participation. Improv provides the opportunity to get more people involved in ministry, whether they think they are "gifted" or not. Your improvs may simply use the audience for suggestions for your actors, or you may actually choose your actors from the audience. There's room here for everybody.

2. You may discover some great talent in your group you didn't know existed. You may have writers and directors in your group, and this gives them a chance to shine. Put them in charge of the improvs and watch them bloom!

3. People love to watch and be a part of something unique, and improv is never the same twice. The more audience members you get involved, the more creative your improvs will be.

4. If you develop a good improv team, your audience will come back to see what your actors come up with next. Also, the people who leave your meeting talking about what they saw may come back looking for an opportunity to get in on the fun.

5. Improv helps present Bible stories in an incredibly fun and creative way. It can teach your audience to read the Bible in a different light, as well as help them better understand that the people in those stories were real and the Bible is relevant in students' lives today.

6. Improv builds confidence within your students. Once your actors develop their improv skills, they will begin to see how creative they can be in making up skits or coming up with funny or dramatic lines.

7. Improv gives students who may have a hard time talking to friends about their faith a platform from which to reach out to those around them.

8. Improv encourages cooperation. This is a great way to help the students in your group work on their scriptwriting skills together as they prepare a skit that could impact their friends' lives in a positive way.

9. Improv develops students' quick-thinking abilities and grounds them in biblical truth—skills they can use when they're presented with an opportunity to share the gospel.

10. Improv gives students a chance to share things about themselves—even things they may not be planning to share. If you watch carefully, you could learn a lot about the hurts, pains, hopes, and dreams of the students who participate in your improvs.

But the main reason to consider using improvs is that the audience gets to see an instant scene. Improvs communicate the main point to the audience in a different way. The best improvs are *real life, real time,* and *real relevance,* as true-to-life stories are given the opportunity to come alive onstage. Improvs can also be used to help set up and/or drive home a speaker's message. Whether they're done on-the-spot or given thought in advance, improvs are a hit, because the actors can use things they've actually experienced or witnessed.

In the pages that follow, you'll find several different tools created for groups just like yours. While some are designed to get you started or help you finish, others are included to help hone your skills in the art of improv. To help you better understand how to use the different parts of this book, let us explain them to you.

TOP TEN IMPROV GAMES

Each one of these games has the potential to help your actors improve their improvisational and acting skills. Some games can be played as teams; some are individual exercises. Some have no point at all, while others can be used to make a point. You can utilize these games in a competitive way or simply for enjoyment. The one thing all the games have in common is that everyone participating will have a great time. Use these games to set up your message or as an alternative to the regular games you may play. You may want to use these games in place of your usual recreation to give your drama kids a chance to shine for a change. However you use these games, just have fun!

SCRIPTURE SKITS

Can you use the Bible to make up improvs and still keep your religious convictions intact? We think so. If you're willing to take that chance, we're willing to help you learn. We'll teach you to use words from the greatest script ever written in order to present wonderful visuals. You'll find 30 passages of Scripture you can read, cast the characters for, and act out in different modes (e.g., traditional King James style, modern, redneck, another language, etc.). Use "Scripture Skits" to take stories you may have heard hundreds of times and bring out new lessons and fresh insights.

PICTURE SKITS

These are the easiest way to get your group involved in improvs. This chapter contains 25 reproducible pictures you can use to get some great improvs going. In this chapter, we teach you two different ways to use "Picture Skits": "What's Going On" and "What If." Both styles are fun and will help bring out creativity in your actors.

GOING SOLO

As you may have guessed, this chapter covers the art of improvisational monologues. (For those of you who thought it would have something to do with Star Wars trivia, please take this book back to the store for a refund. The force is not with you.) Some of the most powerful moments in any play, movie, or television show can be found in a monologue. Here is your chance to create one of those memorable moments with your group. And don't worry—no matter how bad your actors are, we've found that every church has at least one good actor. It may not be someone destined for Broadway, but every church has at least one person who's pretty good in front of a crowd.

CHARACTER CONFLICTS

The toughest part of creating an improv is coming up with the premise. Guess what…We've already done that for you! In fact, we've come up with 120 different ideas for improvs and called them "Character Conflicts." You'll find conflicts about dating, family, work, believers/seekers, school, friendships, taboo subjects, sin issues, and some that are just for fun. Think of these "Character Conflicts" like you think of your bathroom plunger: to use when your creativity is stuck. That's probably a bit gross, but it gets the point across, right?

SCENARIOS

This is probably the most unique section in the book. You'll want to refer to it quickly and often. Here we have the "nuts and bolts" you'll need to put together hundreds of improvs. You'll find all sorts of great lists to get your creative juices flowing; in fact, this will likely become the most-used part of your book. "Scenarios" contains the keys to keeping your improvs fresh and different, so you'll find yourself coming back to this chapter again and again.

Now that you know what to expect from *Instant Skits,* all you need to do is get your actors, wannabe actors, and reformed mimes onstage and let the improvs begin. Wouldn't it be great if it really were that simple? Well, it almost is. But before continuing, let's first go through some improv tips. Read these carefully so you'll be ready for what's about to happen.

ESSENTIAL IMPROV TIPS

APPROPRIATENESS

Make sure you stress the importance of appropriate words and actions in the skit. With any kind of acting—but especially with improv—you never know what's going to come out of someone's mouth, so be ready for someone to say or do something that might be inappropriate. If (or maybe we should say when) this does happen, we recommend a couple of things:

First, don't freak out. You don't want to be the stereotypical adult who immediately condemns every wrongdoing teen. Keep your cool and look for ways to encourage the improv actor, while taking the time to add something like, "I don't know if I would've said it that way," or, "That was a unique way of expressing yourself." The key is to defuse the situation before it blows up on you.

Second, don't act like it didn't happen. If you do nothing, invariably someone will think you're okay with the inappropriateness—and you will hear about it. You will experience some improv moments with young people when you'd love to hide or go back in time and keep it from happening, but they'll happen nonetheless, so you must take care of it.

Please don't let this scare you. Ninety-nine times out of a hundred, everything will be fine. You just want to be prepared for that one percent so you're not caught off-guard.

BAD ACTORS

When choosing audience members to participate in your improvs, you can get some great actors who bring energy and creativity to the stage—and you can get some people who can't act their way out of a paper bag. Trust us, there are few things more grueling than watching someone try to act who can't. Be prepared to encourage the stinkers by always having some ideas in mind to help your volunteers get things going and keep things going.

For example, if Sally and Stephen are trying to improv a scene together and Stephen is stinking it up, here's something you can do: Stand up and say, "Freeze! Aren't Sally and Stephen doing a great job? (Prompt your audience to applaud.) Now, let's try something different. Stephen, I want you to sit down and see how someone else would interpret what you've already started." Now, find another willing participant to take over where Stephen left off and see what happens. If you are worried about Stephen's feelings being hurt, then have both actors sit down and start with two new actors.

This may be a little scary at first, but it won't be half as scary as continuing to sit through a bad improv. You'll also want to keep in mind that what you don't like, your audience may be okay with. People love to watch their peers onstage, and many times they will give them the benefit of the doubt. As the leader, your job is to keep one eye on the stage and the other on the audience to see if you need to intervene.

SAME OLD, SAME OLD

If you use the same group of actors each time, your improvs may start to look very similar. This is of particular concern if you use a specific improv group in a performance-based medium or if your group is too small to use several different people each time. If your group doesn't fall into one of those categories, we encourage you to use as many different people as you can. It's scary to try out new people when you have a good team in place, but you never know who's just waiting to surprise you with incredible talents. Using different actors will help keep your improvs fresh.

If you are using the same group of improv actors each week, try mixing things up with these ideas: 1) Cast your actors in different roles. If you have an actor who always plays the mother-type role, cast her as the daughter for a change. For that matter, cast her as the villain or comedy relief or as the dad even. 2) Help your group by choosing settings and characters that are different from the last time. Don't let it always be in a school or at the mall or in a bathroom. Take your actors outside of their regular setting and see what they can do. What if you place them in a zoo or a bar or a space station? Whatever you do, be creative! (See "Scenarios," section 7.0, to avoid "ruts.")

BAD THEOLOGY

More than likely, some of your groups are going to mess up a biblical passage or two by adding their own interpretation. Don't get too wound up about it; theologians have been doing that for years! Seriously, we want to encourage you to use this theological litmus test for your drama, especially the improvs: "Unity in the essentials, diversity in the non-essentials, and grace in all things."

Since some of the essentials will likely develop, let us give you some practical ideas on how to deal with a biblical blunder or theological faux pas. The key is to correct mistakes in a manner that doesn't make the actors feel ignorant. Never say something like, "Although Cindy was very funny in her improv, you need to know that Moses didn't build an ark; that was Noah." If you do that, not only will Cindy never be in an improv again, she may not come back to your church again.

We suggest you find a more encouraging way to correct her. Try something like, "Wasn't Cindy great? I loved it when her character thought it was Moses who was in the ark instead of Noah. What I loved about it is that sometimes in my life, I've gotten confused about things that happened in the Bible. Let's be honest, when Moses had the Ark of the Covenant and Noah had the ark with the animals, it's easy to see how someone could get confused. Cindy, thanks for showing us that; it was really great!"

If your actor makes a theological statement that goes against your group's belief system, you may want to say something like, "Some people agree with what Doug's character said about God. However, we believe…" In doing this, you have not pointed out Doug's beliefs, but his character's beliefs.

Above all else, figure out a way to encourage your improv actors if you have to correct them. This is a great way to teach them and build them up.

REALISM

If your group is the typical drama group, they may overact—creating skits that only "drama people" think are good. Make sure you discuss with them the importance of using realistic dialogue and actions so they can produce something everyone will enjoy.

Many times when people get up in front of a group to perform, they overdo things. They may tend to over-articulate when they talk, make exaggerated gestures, or walk like an English butler for no reason at all. The key here is to help your improv actors remember that they're not doing theater. These are improvs, or "skits," which are different from theater. What you're looking for is a little slice of life. Help them to be as real as they can be. They may be portraying someone totally different from themselves, but have them do all they can to express that character in a more realistic way.

Similarly, many church skits or improvs can tend to go straight to the "Bible answers" and come across as very unrealistic. Let's be honest—we don't generally say to our neighbor, "The Bible says, 'Thou shall not covet thy neighbor's donkey.' So, my friend, find contentment in what you have." However, we might say, "I know it's tough to look around at what other people have and not get wrapped up in wanting the same things. Sometimes life seems unfair that way. You know what? I've just had to come to the realization that I have everything I need, and I'm not going to worry about trying to keep up with everyone else." So be careful to avoid the "churchy" response. It's often the most unrealistic response for audience members, especially those who may not be Christians.

THEY'RE WATCHING

Remember—you're being watched. Oh, sure, improv is fun—and no doubt your group's very presence on the stage is entertaining. However, always remember that what you're doing has to make sense to the audience. Just as no one wants to sit and watch someone drive a car in circles in a parking lot, no one wants to watch an improv that's not going somewhere.

Here are some things to keep in mind to help your group be more entertaining in their presentations:

1. Think before you speak. Too many people in life tend to just open their mouths and let things come out. In your improvs, try to let everything you say have a purpose. While that doesn't mean each thing you say needs to be a mini-sermon, make sure it's pertinent to what's progressing in the improv.

2. Always see your improv as moving forward toward an unknown destination. We say "unknown" because your audience doesn't know the destination and neither do the actors. However, just as we don't always know our destinations in life, we keep moving forward, discovering what comes next.

If your actors can keep these two things in mind, you'll see your improv actors become far more entertaining and effective in sharing a message.

ALL ABOUT ME

It seems all actors think what they have to say is the most important thing for everyone else to hear. They often spend most of their time thinking about what they can say next; because they want to be the funniest, most clever, or most poignant. This can make for a schizophrenic improv experience.

But good improv is a team sport. Actors must listen to one another if they want to create great skits. Improvisation, like other forms of acting, is less about what or how you say something individually and more about how you respond to those around you. Like a good tennis match, the audience's interest is highest when the ball continues to be hit back and forth. Actors don't want to squelch things other actors toss their way; the challenge is to search for ways to move forward with whatever you're given. Listen to each other and respond appropriately according to your character. If you do, then your improv will progress naturally in the same direction.

STUCK IN A RUT

Don't get stuck in a rut saying the same thing over and over again. Don't get stuck in a rut saying the same thing over and over again. Don't get stuck in a rut saying the same thing over and over again.

Normally this happens when your improv actors aren't thinking. Just as saying the same thing over and over again is unacceptable in life, help your improv actors understand that it is unacceptable on stage. Much of this goes back to listening more than trying to be heard. Think "resolution," "compromise," and "accomplishment." Through these three goals, improvs can be transformed from mediocre to excellent.

SKIT OR MOMENT?

Just like a good story, every good improv has characters, conflict, and a conclusion. As simple as that sounds, it's true that if it doesn't have those elements, it's not a story; it's a moment. The real problem is, most improvs miss out on this idea. They get to a certain point where no one seems to know what to do, so they end abruptly. The key is to let the audience know who you are and what your conflict is, and then resolve it.

Resolution is the key here. If everyone involved is looking to arrive at a destination together, resolving whatever the issue is, you are more than likely going to take care of your characters, conflict, and conclusion.

However, keep in mind you're not doing a mini-series. There isn't time for deep character development or intricate plots, but rather a scene in which people quickly introduce their characters, encounter a conflict, and come to a conclusion. Most improvs should be able to accomplish this in eight to 10 minutes, and many can do so much quicker. You need to decide what is appropriate for your setting and your group and expect your improv actors to stick to the clock. As the old saying goes, "Always leave them wanting more." To do this, you need to keep it short—trust us, your audience will thank you for it.

BE FEARLESS

Improv can be like herding cats: You may get some scratches, but in the end you have…a whole bunch of cats! Okay, maybe that's not the best illustration. The real point here is to jump in with both feet and see what happens.

As we stated earlier, one of the greatest strengths of improv is the mystery of the unknown—but it's also the scariest part. You may be thinking, "What if this doesn't work for us? What if no one gets involved? What if our improv looks more like a bad soap opera than *Saturday Night Live?*" Well…it just might.

But don't be afraid; just get out there and do your best. You'll never know what God can do through you if you don't take chances.

The book you're holding was created to help you add the creative medium of improv to your group. Improvs can be used to make a point, to take up time, as a competition, or just for fun. You choose how you would like to use the improvs, and we'll help your group succeed at them. So get out there, be creative, make something up that people will remember, and most of all—have fun!

TOP TEN IMPROV GAMES

2.0

The following games will help expand your drama team's ability to think on the move. As your actors become more proficient at these exercises, they will also develop the essentials your team needs to be able to put together and perform on-the-spot skits.

2.1
PROP ME UP, HERE

This fast-paced game is a great way to get your team interested in improv. The main idea behind this game is to see who can come up with the most creative uses for the props; therefore, you'll need to have a good selection of props. Try to have some normal, everyday items, as well as some objects that may be more difficult to identify. You can use the list in section 7.6 to get you started.

Select two or more players to get onstage. Divide the players into two teams. All props should be placed in a box at center stage. At your signal, a player from team one pulls out a prop and has 10 seconds to come up with any application for the item other than the object's intended use. Once finished, the first player hands the prop to a player from team two, who must immediately come up with a different use. When finished, the player from team two will then pass the prop to a different player from team one, who must do the same.

This continues back and forth like a Ping-Pong game until someone can't come up with a new idea. Whichever team can't come up with a new idea drops the prop, and the other team gets a point. Hand a new prop to the last successful player and continue in the same direction. This game can be a lot of fun and even more intense if you have a good buzzer to go off at the end of 10 seconds each time.

Caution: This game could potentially yield some inappropriate innuendos if you're not careful. We want to encourage you to strongly emphasize the importance of appropriateness to your game players. You may even want to deduct points if teams are overtly inappropriate.

WHO AM I, AND WHAT AM I FEELING?

In this game, the director has made two sets of index cards. One deck describes occupations, and the other deck describes different feelings. One by one, actors pick one card from each deck and then proceed to present a character combining the suggestions from the two cards. The audience then guesses what the two cards held. You can find a list of occupations in section 7.3 and feelings in 7.5 to get you started.

2.3
THE BALL KNOWS ALL

Have your group sit in a circle with any type of round ball. The director gives life to the ball as the group passes the ball around the circle. For example, the director may say the ball is "heavy," and the group acts as if they can hardly lift it. The players can talk to or about the ball; however, they may not use the same words the director used to give life to the ball. This can also be a great game for involving audience members—have them try to guess what the "life of the ball" is.

Here are some ideas to get you started:

- Fire
- Light
- Bright
- Feels like needles
- Knows what you're thinking
- Thinks you're cute
- Thinks you're funny
- Freezing
- Thinks you think you know all about the ball's horrible past
- Feels like thunder
- Heavy
- Funny
- Knows what you did last summer
- Wet
- Slimy
- Smells like poo
- Allows you to see the future
- Feels like Jell-O™
- Feels like a warm blanket
- Prickly
- Feels like razor blades
- Light as a feather

- Stiff as a board
- Looks like your favorite dessert
- Makes you have allergies
- Sticks to your hands
- Filled with helium
- Splashes on you when you catch it
- Causes you to shout your feelings
- Causes you to laugh
- Causes you to cry
- Causes you to stop breathing until you get rid of it
- Causes you to freeze everything except your arms
- Fluffy like cotton balls
- Causes you to start singing your favorite songs

CHARACTERS, CONFLICTS, & LINES (OH MY!)

Choose a character from section 7.2, a conflict setting from 7.1, and a line to get you going from 7.8 or line to end with from 7.9. Now have your improv players create a scene. To make things more spontaneous, write out the different elements of the scenarios on slips of paper and place them in bowls labeled **characters**, **settings**, and **lines**. Now have your improv players pick from the bowls, read their elements to the audience, and act them out.

Despite the title of the game, the actors aren't actually given a specific conflict. They're simply provided with a person, a place, and a line. Their job is to quickly and creatively develop a character, set up a conflict, and then resolve that conflict.

This is also a great exercise for your actors if you have a regular drama group. If you can get your actors familiar with this format, you'll be on your way to creating great improvs and writing your own skits.

2.5
TRIFECTA

For this game, choose a small group of audience members to be your improv players. Ask them to create an improvisation that must include three specific things: one prop, one line, and one action. For example: The prop may be a roll of toilet paper, the line might be, "Do you ever get the feeling someone is watching you?" and the action could be a somersault. The challenge here is not only using the things you have given them, but also creating an improv that makes sense and has a beginning, middle, and end. You can find a list of props in section 7.6 and some lines to get them going in section 7.8. To help them with this skit, you may also want to provide them with a character and/or setting from the Scenarios section (7.1, 7.2).

2.6
PASS IT ON

Choose three people from the audience to be improv players and have them leave the room. Direct the remaining audience members to come up with a scenario to be acted out. The scenario should include a setting, character, and simple action. (See sections 7.1, 7.2, and 7.7a for some suggestions on these.)

Now, bring the first improv player back into the room. Explain the scenario and tell her to pantomime the scenario for the second improv player. Bring the second improv player in. After the first actor has pantomimed the scenario for the second, bring the third improv player into the room. Have the second improv player pantomime his understanding of the scene as conveyed by the first actor.

Make sure the actors don't speak at all; they should allow the pantomime to convey the message. You also may need to shush the audience at times if people are giving things away through sighs, moans, yelling "no," etc.

Once the second improv player has finished acting out the scenario, ask the third improv player to tell the audience what he thinks the scenario was supposed to be about, including character, location, and situation.

As with the old parlor room game "telephone," each "copy of a copy" loses something in translation—wherein lies the humor for the audience. So feel free to use four or even five actors in the process. And as your group's acting skills progress, feel free to make the scenarios more complicated.

2.7
ASK THE AUDIENCE

This exercise encourages actors to be expressive with their bodies when conveying a scene to the audience. Have members of your drama team act out a scene without using words. The audience should not know what the actors have been assigned to do. After the scene is completed, ask the audience for feedback regarding what they thought the scene was all about. (For suggestions, see the "Slightly More Complex Actions" in section 7.7b.)

2.8

LET'S GO TO THE CLIP

Select several fairly easy scenes from movies. (For help with this game, see any of the *Videos That Teach* books from Youth Specialties.) Cue up the clips and bring them to your event. Show a clip and choose the appropriate number of audience members to re-enact the scene onstage—but with a twist. As the leader, you can go in several different directions, but here are some ideas to get you started:

CRAZY CASTING

Instead of casting the obvious players in roles, mix it up. For example: A large jock could play the role of Mini Me; a small middle school student could play the role of Darth Vader; a male actor could play Julia Roberts, while a female could play Richard Gere.

ALTERNATE ENDING

Although everyone may know how the actual scene ends in the movie, let your actors make up their own ending. Encourage them to be as real or as outrageous as they can be.

OPPOSITES ATTRACT

If the clip you choose is a comedy, have your actors make it a drama, and vice-versa.

MOVIE MAGIC

Instead of showing the clip to your audience, have your improv players leave the room and let them watch the clip in private. Then have them come in and act out the scene for the audience. Have the audience guess what movie it was from. For this game, you may want to meet with your drama group before your event to plan ahead.

2.9

FREEZE FRAME

Choose two to four people from the audience to be your improv players for this game. Next, select another couple of audience members to put the improv players in different positions on the stage. Now ask your audience to come up with ideas for the situation. Pick the one you like, assign characters to your players, and let the improv begin. When you want to change things, shout, "Freeze Frame!" At this signal, your players should freeze where they are and wait for your direction. Now, you have two options:

1) Go back to your audience and let them come up with new ideas for the group in the positions they're in. Start the new improv from here. You can either do this on the fly, or you can have the audience choose several situations before you begin, and every time you yell, "Freeze Frame!" you tell them the new situation from the list you created before the game began.

2) Replace your actors with new improv players and continue the skit, letting the new players put their spin on things.

Feel free to shout, "Freeze Frame!" as much as you want. This is a great way to keep things moving when the improv is going too slow, or to help control the direction things are going when your players get a little too crazy. You'll also find this to be a good way to get audience members involved; they get to watch how improv works while also getting the opportunity to try new things.

2.10
LOOK WHO'S HERE

Quietly assign each player a character and an action (both of which they will keep to themselves). Have your performers take turns getting onstage acting out their characters and actions. You may want to set up a scenario where someone is having a party, and every few minutes, you have a new person come to the party. Once everyone has had the opportunity to perform, ask your audience to guess each player's character and action.

Characters can be famous people or a particular type of person. The action should be something that can be physically acted out and should include anything from a specific action to a certain condition. You can use characters or occupations from sections 7.2 or 7.3 for suggestions, along with traits in 7.4 or simple actions in 7.7a.

SCRIPTURE SKITS

How many times have you watched (and tried to listen) as someone put a group to sleep by reading the Bible like it was a technical manual for a copy machine? That's a shame, isn't it? Because—"It's alive! It's alive!" We need to remember that the Word of God is alive and well, and it presents some wonderful visuals—especially if we can step outside of the way we have always looked at the stories growing up in Sunday school and search for more creative ways to look at them.

"Scripture Skits" are great methods to share passages from God's Word in ways that will make your group laugh, think, and remember what the Bible says. These skits can be as long or as short as you need them to be, and they're bound only by your imagination.

FORMATS

You can present "Scripture Skits" in several different formats:

1. Have the passage read aloud; then let the actors act it out.

2. Have the actors act out the passage as it is read aloud (perhaps like a melodrama).

3. Have the actors act out the passage in place of someone reading it.

4. Have one person read a portion of the passage, allowing the actors to finish it through drama.

PERFORMANCE STYLES

There are also different ways to perform "Scripture Skits." Here are four suggested scenarios:

Audience Scripture Skits

Choose audience members who don't know what passage you're using, and have them come onstage to act out the passage. If the passage is short (or if you have time), feel free to read it aloud one time. Then simply have your volunteers act it out. You may want to make suggestions to your volunteers for different types of characters. You'll also need to decide ahead of time how many characters you'll need in the passage.

Why: Group participation. You get more people involved in the activity, which also leads to greater retention of the message—and more fun!

Improv Scripture Skits

In this scenario, you either use your regular drama group or a group you have chosen in advance that you know has some improv skills. Again, if you have time or if the passage is short, feel free to read it aloud one time before you have the group act it out. Then get suggestions from your audience for characters and settings. Your improv group can then have fun making up their "Scripture Skit" while the audience watches. If time allows, get more ideas from the audience and let your actors go at it again. (Feel free to use some of the improv ideas found in section 2.0, "Top Ten Improv Games," to make this scenario even more creative and fun.)

Why: Great exercise for your experienced actors! This is a good way to bump things up a notch entertainment-wise.

Schizophrenic Scripture Skits

This scenario can be approached in two ways:

Option A

Choose one Scripture passage and turn it over to several groups of students. Give them an overview of the passage (plot, players, point) and have each group leave the room for a moment to collect their thoughts before presenting a spontaneous interpretation of the Scripture. The fun in this scenario comes from seeing how different groups of kids will interpret the same Bible story.

Option B

Break one of the longer passages of Scripture into sections (Jesus and the woman at the well, David and Goliath, and Samson and Delilah are good examples of longer passages than can be subdivided). Divide your students into groups and give each group a section, or scene, of the passage to act out. As each group gets onstage to take over for the other, they have the option of enacting the same characters previously performed by actors from the other group, or they can portray completely new characters who only appear as the story progresses. (Much humor can be derived from seeing the same character personified first by a petite young lady, and moments later by a stocky guy.) Give your students the freedom to choose any characters they wish to represent.

Sometimes your actors know a little more about being funny than they do about theology. In either one of these options, you will want to be ready to gently correct any biblical errors your actors make.

Why: This is a great way to give several different people an opportunity to be involved.

Scripted Scripture Skits

(Try to say that fast five times!) For this type of skit, you give the Scripture passage to your drama group several days in advance and let them read the passage and create a skit out of it. You can make this as structured or as spontaneous as you want. The group may write it down, or just come up with great ideas and lines they want to use. If appropriate, feel free to let them know what you're doing with the passage in your large group teaching or small group discussion time so they can create something that will support what you're doing. Once the time comes for the performance, you can either read the passage aloud before they present their skit, or you can use the skit instead of reading the passage. If the passage is short, encourage your group to come up with two or three different takes on the passage—one funny, one cheesy, and one serious. The more the audience sees the passage acted out, the more they have a chance to let it sink in.

Why: Control, control, control! You know what's going to be said and done, so there are no unwelcome surprises.

KEEP 'EM SHORT

"Scripture Skits" don't need to be too involved or too long. In fact, you may want to do short "Scripture Skits" where your actors present just a small portion of your passage. In those skits, we suggest you have your actors act out the passage a few times, using different types of characters. For example, the story of "The Fall" could first be portrayed like an old biblical movie using "King James" words spoken by your actors. Then you could ask them to present it in a "redneck" format, with the serpent encouraging Eve, for instance, to "git 'er done!" Finally, you may want to change it up and provide a more modern-day presentation to help your audience understand that these were real people just like us.

It's possible that you may not have the time to present your passage in multiple styles. In those situations, just choose the one that best suits the direction you're going with the passage and use it.

A WORD TO THE WISE

The Bible is a holy book containing sacred texts and people whom we honor and respect. Stress to your actors the importance of respecting God's Word by showing reverence in everything they do. It is possible to be funny with a character or even make light of a story in the Bible while still honoring it. If a "Scripture Skit" is presented in the wrong way, it can come across as making fun of the Bible or being sacrilegious. Encourage your actors to be very careful in portraying any image of God. Always keep in mind that the picture you paint of the Father, the Son, or the Holy Spirit may be the only picture some people see of them. We don't mean to scare you away from "Scripture Skits," but we do encourage you to be careful.

SUGGESTED PASSAGES

You can choose almost any passage from the Bible for "Scripture Skits." However, some passages are more difficult to act out (like anything from the book of Lamentations); some aren't really meant for humor (like the crucifixion); and some just leave your actors looking at each other blankly wondering how to act things out (like most of Revelation).

To help save you time, we have listed 30 of our favorite passages to be used for "Scripture Skits," along with suggestions for different character ideas.

3.1
THE FALL

The Passage: Genesis 3:1-24

The Plot: Adam and Eve are influenced by a clever serpent to disobey God's instructions for life in the Garden of Eden.

The Players: Adam, Eve, God, the serpent (Satan)

The Point: Disobedience (obedience), sin, deception, wrath of God, choices, consequences

3.2
THE FLOOD

The Passage: Genesis 6:9-22

The Plot: After realizing the new world he created is full of sin, God finds one righteous man and gives him an unbelievable mission. Giving his servant Noah a list of specific instructions, God prepares a way to wipe out everything he has created and start all over.

The Players: God, Noah, Shem, Ham, Japheth

The Point: Corruption, obedience, trust, faith

3.3
ABRAHAM'S SACRIFICE

The Passage: Genesis 22:1-19

The Plot: God tests his servant Abraham by asking him to sacrifice the son Abraham has waited a lifetime to have. Abraham obeys God, taking Isaac to a holy mountain, preparing to sacrifice him. When God realizes Abraham is willing to give up his long-awaited son, God steps in and provides an alternative.

The Players: Abraham, Isaac, God, a ram

The Point: Trust, obedience, faith, provision of God, blessings

3.4
JACOB'S TWO WIVES

The Passage: Genesis 29:14-30

The Plot: Jacob, after being threatened by his angry brother Esau, has fled to his uncle Laban's house. Once Jacob catches sight of Laban's daughter Rachel, he falls deeply in love with her and strikes a bargain with his uncle to work for him for seven years for the privilege of marrying her. But Laban tricks Jacob, and after Jacob's seven years of labor are completed, Laban instead gives Jacob the older daughter Leah in marriage. Disappointed but not deterred, Jacob agrees to work for Laban seven more years so he can marry the woman he truly loves.

The Players: Laban, Jacob, Leah, Rachel, wedding partiers

The Point: True love, dedication, perseverance, honesty, justice

JACOB'S WRESTLING MATCH

The Passage: Genesis 32:22-32

The Plot: Once again running for his life, Jacob has taken his whole family and is fleeing across the desert. Unable to sleep one night, Jacob meets up with an aggressive stranger, and they begin to wrestle. Though Jacob's opponent—an angel—outmatches him, Jacob fights valiantly and forces the angel to bless him.

The Players: Jacob, the angel, Jacob's two wives, children, servants

The Point: Adversity, perseverance, fear, courage

3.6
BALAAM'S DONKEY

The Passage: Numbers 22:21-38

The Plot: After leaving Egypt, the Israelites are traveling through the land of Moab on their way to the Promised Land. Balak, the king of Moab, has heard news of the Israelites' defeat of the Amorites, so he sends for a man named Balaam to come to Moab and put a curse on the Israelites. When Balaam decides to give in to the Moabites' pleas for help, God allows him to go but is angry with Balaam's decision. To get his message across in an effective way, God gives Balaam's donkey the ability to speak.

The Players: Balaam, a donkey, God, two servants, an angel, Balak, Balak's princes

The Point: Disobedience (obedience), blessing, cursing, protection of God, miracles

3.7

A LEFT-HANDED SAVIOR

The Passage: Judges 3:15-30

The Plot: Israel, in conflict with Moab, cries out to the Lord to send them a deliverer. The Lord gives them Ehud, a left-handed soldier with a special sword. Ehud visits the kingdom of Moab on the pretense of bringing a tribute to Eglon, the hugely fat king of Moab. After managing to clear the room of attendants and servants, Ehud stabs and kills Eglon through the king's rolls of fat, inspiring an uprising of the Israelites against Moab.

The Players: Several Israelites, Ehud, Eglon, attendants, servants, soldiers

The Point: Rescue, courage, bravery, protection of God

3.8
SAMSON AND DELILAH

The Passage: Judges 16:1-22

The Plot: Samson, a longhaired prophet blessed by God with incredible strength, falls in love with a woman named Delilah—one of the dreaded Philistines. When the Philistine rulers realize Samson has been entering their borders to visit Delilah, they recruit her to help them defeat and capture Samson. But Samson is too clever for Delilah's attempts to uncover the source of his strength, until her nagging finally drives him to tell her the truth. While he's sleeping, she cuts the hair he's been growing since birth, and his legendary strength is gone.

The Players: Samson, Delilah, Philistine rulers, Philistine thugs

The Point: Choices, consequences, immorality (sin), lying (honesty), lust

PUNISHMENT FOR A STOLEN ARK

The Passage: 1 Samuel 5:6-12; 6:1-21

The Plot: The Philistines, who have stolen the Ark of the Covenant from the Israelites, have begun to suffer God's wrath in the form of tumors and hemorrhoids. Though they move the ark to several different cities in an effort to avoid God's curse, it follows the ark, and each group of people is afflicted with the outbreak of tumors, hemorrhoids, and rats. The rulers of the Philistines gather together and decide to send the ark back to Israel, along with a guilt offering of golden tumors and golden rats. Following the instructions to place the ark and their golden offerings on a cart pulled by cows, the Philistines send the ark back to Israel in hopes that God will lift the curse and leave them alone.

The Players: Townspeople of Ashdod, townspeople of Gath, townspeople of Ekron, Philistine rulers, priests, townspeople and Levites of Beth Shemesh

The Plot: Consequences, obedience, wrath of God, offerings, defiance

3.10
DAVID CHOSEN BY SAMUEL

The Passage: 1 Samuel 16:1-13

The Plot: Saul, the man chosen by God's prophet Samuel to be Israel's king, has turned out to be a huge disappointment. Though Samuel would rather mourn over Saul's decline, God instructs him to anoint a new king. God sends Samuel to the house of Jesse to choose from Jesse's many sons. As each of Jesse's strong and worthy-looking sons passes before Samuel, he realizes none of them are God's choice, so he asks Jesse to bring out his youngest son, David. Though David is only a teenager herding sheep, God tells Samuel to anoint him with oil, marking David as Israel's new king.

The Players: Samuel, God, a cow, town elders, Jesse, Jesse's seven sons, David, some sheep

The Point: Obedience, trust, appearances, inner worth

3.11

DAVID AND GOLIATH

The Passage: 1 Samuel 17

The Plot: With the Israelite and Philistine armies ready to fight, the Philistines attempt to eat away at the Israelites' courage by sending out their giant warrior Goliath to hurl insults. When Goliath challenges the Israelite army to send out an opponent for him to fight, none of the soldiers are brave enough to accept. While visiting the Israelite camp to bring food to his older brothers, young David hears Goliath's challenge and offers to face the giant. Though the Israelite soldiers laugh at him, David trusts God to be with him as he approaches Goliath and wins a stunning victory.

The Players: Philistine soldiers, Israelite soldiers, Goliath, shield bearer, King Saul, Eliab, Abinadab, Shammah, Jesse, David, Abner

The Point: Courage, faith, protection of God, provision of God, victory

3.12
SOLOMON'S WISE DECISION

The Passage: 1 Kings 3:16-28

The Plot: Two women arguing over a baby approach King Solomon for an answer to their dispute. Solomon, known for his great wisdom, listens to both sides of the argument and proposes an unusual solution, which brings the truth to light.

The Players: Two women, a baby, King Solomon

The Point: Selfishness, wisdom, arguing, compassion

3.13
ELISHA IS JEERED

The Passage: 2 Kings 2:23-25

The Plot: A gang of young boys finds out how dangerous it can be to mess with one of God's prophets. After chasing Elisha and calling him "bald-head," the boys turn tail and run when God sends two bears out of the woods to attack them.

The Players: Several boys, Elisha, two bears

The Point: Respect, protection of God, choices, consequences

3.14
BOY JESUS IN THE TEMPLE

The Passage: Luke 2:41-52

The Plot: As a young boy, Jesus and his family make the annual trip to Jerusalem for the Feast of the Passover. When his parents begin the journey home, they realize Jesus isn't with them, and they rush back to Jerusalem to search for him. After three days, Jesus' parents find him sitting in the temple, discussing the Scriptures with the elders.

The Players: Jesus, Mary, Joseph, fellow travelers, temple elders

The Point: Knowledge of Scripture (Word of God), respect, plan of God

3.15

JESUS AND THE WOMAN AT THE WELL

The Passage: John 4:4-42

The Plot: While traveling through Samaria, Jesus stops at a well for a drink of water. When a Samaritan woman approaches the well, Jesus asks her to draw him some water—a strange request, since Jews and Samaritans are mortal enemies. Jesus offers the woman the living water of salvation and forgiveness, prompting her to run back to her village and spread the word that the Messiah has come.

The Players: Jesus, his disciples, the Samaritan woman, Samaritan villagers

The Point: Forgiveness, salvation, love, witnessing (evangelism)

3.16
THE POOL OF BETHESDA

The Passage: John 5:1-16

The Plot: In Jerusalem is a special pool known as the Pool of Bethesda. According to legend, the first person into the waters after an angel stirs it into motion will be healed of any affliction. Since only one person is healed during each event, many sick, lame, and paralyzed people wait around its edge for their turn to be the first one in. When Jesus visits the pool, he notices a man who has been waiting to get into the water for 38 years. Jesus asks the man if he would like to be healed. Misunderstanding, the man thinks Jesus is offering to help him get into the pool. But Jesus speaks the words of healing, and the man is able to get up and walk, testifying about his miracle.

The Players: Many sick, wounded, or paralyzed people, Jesus, paralyzed man, Jewish leaders

The Point: Healing, faith, gratitude, tradition

3.17
JESUS HEALS A PARALYTIC

The Passage: Luke 5:17-26

The Plot: While Jesus is teaching and healing the sick, a large crowd gathers, including several disbelieving Pharisees. Several friends of a paralyzed man, unable to get through the crowd listening to Jesus' teaching, devise a clever way to get him close to Jesus: They cut a hole in the roof of the house and lower the man down. When Jesus sees their dedication and faith, he heals the man—much to the shock of the Pharisees.

The Players: Jesus, many listeners, several Pharisees, paralyzed man, his friends

The Point: Authority, healing, faith, dedication, forgiveness, miracles, glory of God

3.18
THE PARABLE OF THE SOWER

The Passage: Matthew 13:3-23

The Plot: Jesus tells a story illustrating the different ways people are affected by his message. When the disciples question Jesus' decision to speak to the people in parables, Jesus explains his deeper meaning, helping everyone understand.

The Players: Jesus, crowd of people, several disciples, the sower (farmer), seeds, birds, sun, thorns, healthy plants

The Point: Choices, the gospel, belief (disbelief)

3.19

JESUS CALMS THE STORM

The Passage: Mark 4:35-41

The Plot: Overwhelmed by the crowds of people following them around, Jesus and his disciples decide to take a boat to the other side of a lake. On their way across the water, the disciples face a dangerous storm that blows up suddenly while Jesus is sleeping. The disciples, terrified of the storm, awaken Jesus and beg for help. Jesus exerts his authority over the wind and the waves by telling them to be still.

The Players: Jesus, the disciples

The Point: Authority, storms, trust, faith, protection of God

3.20
JESUS FEEDS THE 5,000

The Passage: John 6:1-15

The Plot: With crowds of people following Jesus to hear him speak, Jesus decides to test his disciples by telling them to find food for the masses. The disciples are at a loss for what to do, until Andrew finds a young boy with a lunch of his own. To the disciples' amazement, Jesus takes five loaves of bread and two fish, blesses them, and produces enough food for the entire crowd of people.

The Players: Jesus, the disciples, crowd of people, young boy

The Point: Miracles, provision, belief, faith

3.21
JESUS WALKS ON WATER

The Passage: Matthew 14:22-36

The Plot: Exhausted from teaching crowds of people for days at a time, Jesus sends his disciples across the lake while he goes off by himself to pray. When evening comes, Jesus decides to rejoin his disciples in an unusual way: He walks out to their boat across the water. The disciples are terrified—until Jesus speaks to them, at which point Peter summons up the courage to step out of the boat. He does, in fact, take a few steps, but quickly gets distracted by the wind and begins to sink. Jesus rescues him, teaching his followers an important lesson about faith.

The Players: Jesus, Peter, other disciples

The Point: Trust, faith, courage, comfort zone, focus

3.22
THE GOOD SAMARITAN

The Passage: Luke 10:25-37

The Plot: In order to answer a question asked by a religious scholar, Jesus tells a story explaining the true meaning of the word "neighbor." To give his story, or parable, more impact, Jesus uses characters who normally would have nothing to do with each other—specifically, a Jewish man and a Samaritan. When the Jew is attacked and wounded by robbers, two Jewish leaders ignore him, walking by without helping. But a Samaritan, his enemy, not only dresses his wounds, but also provides him with safe travel and a place to rest, taking care of the financial needs involved.

The Players: Jesus, religious scholar, Jewish traveler, priest, Levite, Samaritan, innkeeper, some robbers

The Point: Compassion (mercy), prejudice, pride (superiority), love

3.23

JESUS WITH MARY AND MARTHA

The Passage: Luke 10:38-42

The Plot: Jesus and his disciples make a rest-stop on their journey at the home of two sisters, Mary and Martha. Martha, who takes pride in her domestic skills and wants to prepare her home for the visitors, works hard in the kitchen, while her sister Mary sits and listens to Jesus speak. When Martha asks Jesus to reprimand Mary for not helping her, Jesus tells her that spending time with him is more valuable than any work to be done.

The Players: Jesus, the disciples, Mary, Martha

The Point: Priorities, selfishness, worry, pride, focus

3.24
THE PRODIGAL SON

The Passage: Luke 15:11-32

The Plot: A selfish young man, wanting to live a more exciting life, asks his father to go ahead and give him his inheritance. The young man quickly wastes all of the money and finds himself at rock bottom, sharing food with hogs. When he decides to face his father and return home, he is greeted and welcomed by his father, angering the older brother, who stayed behind to work the entire time.

The Players: Young man, father, older brother, partying friends, hog farmer, father's servants

The Point: Selfishness, forgiveness, stewardship, bitterness, love

3.25

JESUS AND THE 10 LEPERS

The Passage: Luke 17:11-19

The Plot: Jesus, traveling to Jerusalem, comes across 10 men with leprosy. Knowing who Jesus is, the lepers cry out to him, asking for healing and mercy. Jesus instructs them to show themselves to the village priests, and while they are on their way to do so, they are cleansed from their leprosy. When one of the men, a Samaritan, realizes he has been healed, he's overwhelmed with gratitude and rushes back to thank Jesus. Jesus is pleased with him but simultaneously disappointed that only one man returned to thank him.

The Players: Jesus, 10 lepers

The Point: Gratitude, faith, forgiveness, healing, mercy

3.26
THE RICH YOUNG MAN

The Passage: Matthew 19:16-30

The Plot: An earnest young man quizzes Jesus about what it takes to gain eternal life. When Jesus tells him to keep God's commandments, the young man is pleased—until Jesus tells him to sell his possessions and give to the poor in order to have treasure in heaven. Being very wealthy, the young man is disappointed and walks away from salvation.

The Players: Jesus, rich young man, disciples, Peter

The Point: Priorities, selfishness, materialism, sacrifice, idolatry

ZACCHAEUS

The Passage: Luke 19:1-10

The Plot: While traveling through Jericho, Jesus and his disciples are mobbed by crowds of people. Tax collector Zacchaeus desperately wants to see Jesus and comes up with a plan to overcome his lack of height: He climbs up a tree to see over the heads of those around him. He is shocked, however, when Jesus walks by, addresses him by name, and invites himself to Zacchaeus' house.

The Players: Zacchaeus, townspeople, a tree, Jesus, disciples

The Point: Forgiveness, reputation, cheating, stealing

3.28
JESUS RAISES LAZARUS FROM THE DEAD

The Passage: John 11:1-44

The Plot: Jesus returns to the home of his friends Mary and Martha after they summon him to help their sick brother. But Jesus waits a few days, and when he finally arrives, Lazarus has died. The sisters are confused and hurt. Jesus demonstrates God's incredible power by bringing Lazarus back to life.

The Players: Jesus, the disciples, Mary, Martha, townspeople, Lazarus

The Point: Miracles, grief, glory of God, plan of God

3.29

THE PARABLE OF THE TALENTS

The Passage: Matthew 25:14-30

The Plot: A wealthy landowner with many servants goes on a journey, giving responsibilities to three of his servants. To one servant, he gives 5,000 dollars, to another servant, 2,000, and to a third servant, 1,000. The first servant, wanting to please his master, goes to work and doubles his master's money, as does the second servant. But the third servant, fearing his master, buries the money to keep it safe. When the master returns, he's pleased with his first two servants and angry with the lazy third servant who chose not to go out on a limb.

The Players: Rich man, three servants

The Point: Work, laziness (complacency), responsibility, fear

3.30
A BOY AND A WINDOW

The Passage: Acts 20:7-12

The Plot: While the apostle Paul is speaking at a house full of people, a young man named Eutychus falls asleep while sitting in an open window. Eutychus falls out of the window to his death as Paul is talking. In the excitement following the accident, Paul runs outside to see what has happened. Paul throws himself across Eutychus, and, to everyone's amazement, Eutychus is brought back to life.

The Players: Paul, townspeople, Eutychus

The Point: Healing, belief, glory of God, miracles

4.0 PICTURE SKITS

"If a picture paints a thousand words, then why can't I write a skit?"

Have you ever looked at a picture and wondered about the story behind it? Better yet, have you ever looked at a picture and *made up* the story behind it? If so, you can write a skit. It really can be that easy. In this exercise, you use pictures and let your students make up the stories for them.

The idea is to find a picture of people doing something, choose the appropriate number of improv actors, and put them in the same positions as the people in the picture. The goal of the actors, then, is to create a skit that begins with people in those positions.

If your group is small enough, pass the picture around the audience so everyone can see it. You can also show the picture to your audience on a big screen or TV as your actors are getting into place. If neither one of those works for you, then just explain the picture to the audience. Your audience will enjoy the improv more if they understand why the actors are starting in this position.

To help get you started, we've provided 25 pictures at the end of this chapter, but please feel free to use your own pictures. You can use pictures from newspapers, magazines, children's books, past group events, movie posters, the Internet—anywhere. If you're letting others choose pictures, be sure to screen all of them first to make sure they're appropriate for what you're doing.

TYPES OF PICTURE SKITS

You can do this a couple of different ways:

What's Going On Here?

In this "Picture Skit," your actors assume the same positions as the people in the picture; then they decide what happens next. You want your actors to take on the roles of the people in the pictures and finish the story.

For example, if you had a picture of four cheerleaders at a football game, then you would choose four actors to assume the positions of the cheerleaders and then act out what they think is going on and what might happen next. Maybe one of the cheerleaders forgets the cheer, and the humor of the skit comes from watching her try to follow all the other cheerleaders. Maybe the football team is playing so badly that the cheerleaders begin to make up new cheers about how bad their team is. Maybe the cheerleaders are ignoring the football team and are cheering for an individual on the sidelines who's trying to do some menial task, like sweeping up candy wrappers.

You may also want to mix up your casting in this kind of skit by putting four big jocks in the role of the cheerleaders.

What If?

In this "Picture Skit," just like in the one above, your actors assume the same positions as the people in the picture and then decide what happens next. But there's a twist—the actors can be doing anything *except* what the people in the picture are actually doing.

For example, let's go back to our picture of the cheerleaders. Now your actors can *not* be cheerleaders, and they can not be doing cheers. Maybe they're at a protest yelling about something. Maybe they're giving directions to someone who's hanging a picture or moving furniture. Maybe they're four people in cold weather jumping up and down trying to stay warm.

USES OF PICTURE SKITS

"Picture Skits" can be used for setting up your message, training your drama group, or just for fun. Here are some tips for using them in each of those situations.

Setting Up Your Message

With the topic of your message in mind, pick one to three pictures that lend themselves to that subject. Now use either volunteers or your drama team to act out "Picture Skits." You may want to let them know what your theme is so they can reinforce the message. Feel free to give participants the points to your message and any key words you would want them to use.

Training Your Drama Group

"Picture Skits" are great for stirring up the creative juices of your drama group. When using "What's Going On Here," challenge your students to think outside the box. Find out who can come up with the craziest situation, the most creative situation, and the most realistic situation. Of course, "Picture Skits" lend themselves to humor, but they are also great for helping your actors learn to create "real life" skits that can drive home great messages.

When using "What If," try to see how many different situations your group can come up with using just one picture. As you use "Picture Skits" to help develop creativity and improvisational skills, make sure to write down the ideas they come up with for use in future skits.

Just for Fun

Have three to six pictures ready to go, depending on the amount of time you have. Let your crowd know what you're getting ready to do; then call for volunteers from the audience. Show the picture to your volunteers and audience, and then turn them loose. As you would with any kind of audience-participation improv, be ready for just about anything to happen. This can be a great time for getting to know people better and discovering "hidden talent" within your group.

PICTURES FOR PICTURE SKITS

Please feel free to use the following pictures to get started using "Picture Skits." You may want to scan them to project the pictures for your audience or go to www.youthspecialties.com/store/downloads password: skitsejtw to download digital copies of the pictures.

Three People

One putting hands over mouth, one putting hand over ears, one putting hand over eyes.

Two People

② Guy picking up girl like they are about to go through a door like on a honeymoon.

3   **One Person**
Scratching their head with one finger and other hand on hips.

4 **Two People**
Standing on top of chairs with both of their arms spread out real wide.

Three People

One person bent over holding stomach, other person grabbing their hair, the other person looks as if to say, "Don't panic!"

5

 6

Four People
Two people standing with the other two on their backs/piggy back style.
Looking different directions/all faces looking different directions.

<table>
<tr><td>**7**</td><td>**Two People**
Sitting down, look like they are both laughing hysterically.</td></tr>
</table>

8   **Five People**
Pointing to the same object.

9
Two People
One person looks like they are climbing out a window, the other looks surprised.

Three People

10 They look like they are all in a fight with each other. One person with hands up in the air, one person with hands on head in disgust, the other with hands on hips or arms folded.

Three People

11 One person is on all fours, one person looks like a chicken, the other is sitting on knees with hands to his cheeks like fins on a fish.

Six People

12 Looks like they are in a stadium cheering on a football game. Have each person do something different with arms and body expressions.

	Two People
13	Facing each other with fingers interlocked like they are playing a game of "Mercy."

	Two People
14	Wrestling.

15	**Six People**
	All in different stretching positions.

	Four People
16	Clicking glasses together in a toast.

 17

Two People
Looking around with hand over eyebrows to shield the sun.

	Three People
18	Doing the "Hokey Pokey."

19

Six People
Making a pyramid.

	Five People
20	Four people singing and one person directing them.

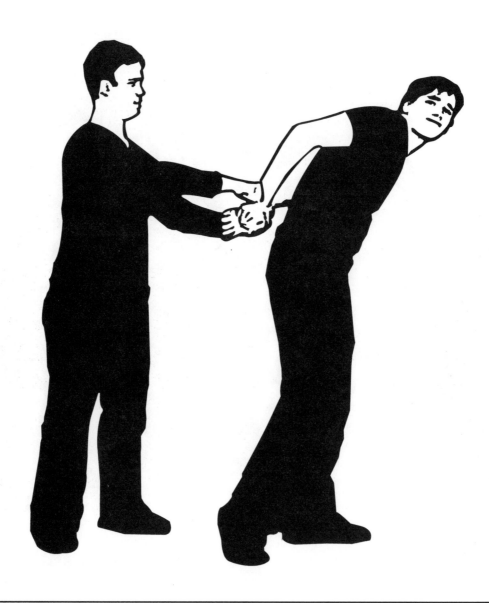

21	**Two People**
	One with hands behind their back as if handcuffed and the other one holding them by the arm like a cop.

	Two People
22	Sitting at a table looking at each other.

	One Person
23	Standing straight with hand over heart.

	Six People
24	Sitting in chairs volunteering with hand in the air.

	Two People
25	Standing with hands on their hips, looking at the camera.

5.0
GOING SOLO

It has been said that every church has at least one good actor. (If you're thinking you've heard that somewhere before, you're right, you have—from us! If you haven't heard that before, go back and read the introduction to this book like you should have. It was a ton of work writing that thing!) Seriously, though—just as every church feels like they have one person who can belt out a Sandi Patty song better than the original, almost every church thinks at least one of their members is an actor.

If you're in that kind of situation—where you have one "good" actor—then you may want to consider improv monologues for your group. Seriously, one of the best challenges for any actor is to be on-stage by himself trying to create something from nothing without any outside support. It's like walking the tightrope without a net. Although it's much scarier for an actor, it can also be much more entertaining—that is, if he doesn't fall!

To help your actors stay on that tightrope, share the ABCs of Monologue Improvs with them.

A

Act like a real person. Remember, you're trying to connect with the audience and teach them something, so don't try to look like a Julliard-trained, Emmy Award-seeking soap opera reject cast in an after-school special. Just be real. Even the most outlandish of characters and situations can have a sense of realism to them. Audiences tend to connect better when they can relate to the characters they're watching.

B

Be careful, or you'll find yourself droning on and on and on and on— you get the picture. One major struggle with monologues is that you don't have anyone onstage to bounce things off of or to keep you in check. If you're not careful, you can find yourself wandering from the subject at hand. Even if you have the ability to spin stories like a war hero with a captive audience, just say what you need to say and sit down.

C

Create a moment for your audience. More than anything, monologues are used to create a brief moment for the audience. As the character, you're letting the audience into your head and heart. Open up, think about real situations you've encountered, and use that emotion and energy to communicate with more than words. Tug at their hearts, make them think, and make them laugh. If you can do that, you'll create a moment in time they won't quickly forget.

So, keeping these things in mind, take one of the 50 scenarios we've created just for monologues in section 5.1 and create a memorable moment. Remember, one of the best challenges for an actor is to be onstage alone with the goal of creating something from within. Try these monologues once your team has been through some sketches together and feels comfortable around one another. By the way, some of these improvisational monologues may turn out to be great skits, too.

The following games will help expand your drama team's ability to think on the move. As your actors become more proficient at these exercises, they will also develop the essentials your team needs to be able to put together and perform on-the-spot skits.

5.1
MONOLOGUE MOMENTS

1. Student talking about the break-up of a relationship.
2. Middle schooler talking about the death of someone close to her.
3. High schooler asking someone out on a date.
4. Young adult confronting a school bully from the past.
5. High school senior sharing the story of being dumped the night before the prom.
6. Poor woman explaining how working at a fast-food chain has changed her life.
7. Parent telling a child about something he learned from that child.
8. Person on a job interview just minutes after coming from the dentist's office.
9. Child sharing about a Christmas when there wasn't much under the tree.
10. Older adult looking back on her life.
11. Parent telling a child "no" and explaining "why."
12. Guy sharing about the best day of his life.
13. Girl sharing about the worst day of her life.
14. High schooler sharing about the night he got drunk or experimented with drugs and the consequences that followed.
15. College student sharing about losing her virginity and the consequences.
16. Actor in a Shakespearean play who hasn't memorized any of his lines.
17. Student rationalizing why she cheated on the Spanish quiz.
18. Homeless person sharing his view of his world versus your world.
19. Most boring person on the planet giving a graduation speech.
20. Flight attendant trying to keep people calm during turbulence on an airplane.
21. _____ (pick a character from section 7.2) imparting the meaning of life.
22. Person on his deathbed talking about his regrets in life.
23. Student talking about being lonely on a daily basis at school.
24. Student talking about leaving home to do something great with her life.
25. Young kid talking about his older brother or sister and how much he looks up to him or her.
26. Person sharing about the worst date he ever had and how it included the passing of gas.

27. Student worrying about how the "B" on her report card will not be acceptable to her performance-driven parents.
28. Teenager lamenting about how badly a much-anticipated date went.
29. Student comparing life to a game of dodge ball at school.
30. Freshman telling the story of a suicide, revealing in the end that she is the person who committed suicide.
31. College student explaining how great his job is (cleaning up after animals at the circus).
32. Person explaining how her medical condition causes her to yell at inappropriate times, but the medication seems to be working (actor yells for no reason while telling the story).
33. High school graduate reflecting on going to war right out of high school: Why did it happen, and was it worth it?
34. Person asking the question: If God is real, why did this happen?
35. Geek explaining in a technical way how love works.
36. Bus driver explaining the "joys" of taking kids to the one place in the world they don't want to go.
37. Person telling the story of the blind guy who tried to give him directions on how to drive.
38. Young middle schooler explaining how she is going to marry a famous person and why he will fall in love with her.
39. Teenager sharing about an incident that changed his life forever.
40. Friend asking another if he can tell him a secret about a part of his life.
41. Atheist giving reasons why believing in Christ seems so "messed up."
42. Person in one of your classes sharing that even though you don't know she exists, she watches how you live out your life as you proclaim to be a Christian.
43. Person claiming to be the strongest human alive, but each time he touches a part of his body, he winces in pain.
44. Person asking someone else what it's like to be popular/beautiful/smart, then relaying why she's never felt that attribute and the reasons why.
45. Convict, surrounded by police, calling his parents on their cell phone to say goodbye.
46. CEO of a large corporation telling her workers she's going to downsize—but who has "laughing fits" for no apparent reason.
47. Person talking about being happy with himself, but instead of talking, he raps everything.
48. First grader talking about her first bus ride home.
49. Person praying and wanting to trust God but having trouble figuring out what that looks like.
50. Person trying to talk himself out of being attracted to someone at school.

CHARACTER CONFLICTS

Inevitably, the most difficult part of creating improvs is coming up with the premise. The following pages contain 120 different improv ideas. To make it easier for you to find what you need, we've divided the "Character Conflicts" into 10 different categories:

1. Dating Conflicts
2. Family Conflicts
3. Work Conflicts
4. Believer/Seeker Conflicts
5. School Conflicts
6. Friendship Conflicts
7. Taboo Conflicts
8. Faith Conflicts
9. Sin Conflicts
10. Just For Fun Conflicts

"Character Conflicts" provide a basic outline for an improv through the following elements:

Situation: The main idea of the improv

Conflict: Outlines the setting, characters, and conflict to be portrayed

Spice It Up: Offers an option to take the improv in a different direction

Themes: Suggested topics that can be addressed through the improv

Actors: The number of actors needed for the improv

"Character Conflicts" are a great way to get any improv started or to use as ideas to write a skit. They can help your actors create improvs dealing with specific subjects, which will come in handy if you want to convey a particular message to the audience.

To use "Character Conflicts," find the conflict you want to use, choose the appropriate number of actors, and get started. Please note that many of the gender roles in each "Character Conflict" are flexible. Casting is at the discretion of the director or leader.

6.1
DATING CONFLICTS

6.1A

Situation: Heartbreak in the ladies' room

Conflict: Girl runs into the restroom crying because her boyfriend said something hurtful. Two of her friends follow her into the ladies' room and attempt to console her.

Spice It Up: Once the girls have developed the skit, have the boyfriend show up outside the restroom and try to talk to her through the door, asking her to come out.

Themes: Broken heart, relationships, hurt, arguing

Actors: Two or three girls (*Spice It Up*: One additional guy)

6.1B

Situation: Encouragement in the men's room

Conflict: Guy paces the bathroom floor trying to summon the courage to ask a girl out. His buddy walks in and starts to help him by role-playing the part of the girl.

Spice It Up: Another guy walks into the restroom, catching the two buddies in an awkward moment. Or have the girl enter the men's restroom by mistake and hear her name spoken.

Themes: Courage, insecurities, dating, inner worth, fear, awkward situations

Actors: Two guys (*Spice It Up*: One additional girl or one additional guy)

6.1C

Situation: If I were to rate that one on a scale from 1 to 10…

Conflict: It's the beginning of the new school year. Two or three buddies are checking out the new "babes" on campus. (Maybe the guys are total geeks and obviously don't stand a chance with the girls they are checking out.)

Spice It Up: Have a couple of the girls overhear them and be offended by the talk.

Themes: Respect, lust, appearance, gossip

Actors: Two or three guys (*Spice It Up*: Two or three additional girls)

6.1D

Situation: Like, we have to talk…I've got some news…

Conflict: Two best friends have some news to tell one another about the guys they like. Actor 1 mentions a guy in one of her classes at school who she has a crush on. She never mentions a name, but as she describes the guy, Actor 2 realizes her friend is talking about her own new boyfriend of one week.

Spice It Up: The guy approaches. At this point, Actor 2 introduces the guy as her new boyfriend.

Themes: Friendship, relationships, honesty, embarrassment, awkward situations

Actors: Two girls (*Spice It Up:* One additional guy)

6.1E

Situation: Dude, where's my wallet?

Conflict: Two couples are at dinner together. When the girls excuse themselves from the table, one of the guys confesses he needs help paying the bill because he forgot his wallet. The second guy agrees to help him out but realizes he also forgot his wallet. Just then, the girls come back from the restroom.

Themes: Dating, awkward situations, honesty, integrity

Actors: Two guys and two girls

6.1F

Situation: Um, I'm late…and I don't mean for dinner.

Conflict: Guy and girl are sitting next to each other waiting on the results of a pregnancy test. As they wait, they discuss their options if she is pregnant. They also discuss the reasons they wanted to have sex in the first place.

Spice It Up: Both of them look at the test. We don't get to see the results. Are they pregnant or not? What choices do they make once we know the result?

Themes: Premarital sex, responsibility, relationships, choices, consequences, true love

Actors: One guy and one girl

6.1G

Situation: May I have this dance?

Conflict: Girl has been asked to a dance by two guys and has said yes to both of them. Audience sees girl work both sides of the room to appease her two dates. The two guys are very different from one another. When they realize what is going on, they confront the girl.

Spice It Up: Switch parts. Have a guy be the one going back and forth with two girls.

Themes: Dishonesty, selfishness, pride, deception

Actors: One girl and two guys (*Spice It Up:* One guy and two girls)

6.1H

Situation: The Dating Game

Conflict: Use the classic Dating Game format: one host, one interviewer, and three contestants. The interviewer asks two different questions about dating to each contestant. Each of the three contestants is a different character. Remember: The interviewer cannot see the contestants and must choose one of them at the end of the game.

Themes: Character, dating, choices, competition

Actors: One host and either one girl and three guys OR one guy and three girls

6.1I

Situation: DTR talk

Conflict: Boyfriend and girlfriend sit down to have a "Define the Relationship" talk. Boyfriend wants to get more serious and physical and not date anyone else; girl is willing to get more serious emotionally but doesn't want to go any further physically.

Spice It Up: Both are believers. Where do they go with the relationship? Or play it where neither of the actors has a walk with God. Where does it end up? Or switch parts in the conflict itself. Why would the girl want to get more physical?

Themes: Boundaries, relationships, breaking up, feelings

Actors: One guy and one girl

6.1J

Situation: The famous final scene

Conflict: The relationship is over and has been for quite a while. The couple meets one last time to put closure on their once wonderful relationship. As they talk, they start discussing how things went from amazing to awful, including how each dealt with certain problems and character traits that weren't so pleasant to the other.

Themes: Honesty, differences, feelings, future, breaking up

Actors: One guy and one girl

6.1K

Situation: Is our love long-term?

Conflict: With graduation approaching, two high school seniors really care for each other. They talk about what they want for their futures and their relationship after high school is over.

Spice it Up: Believing that if they are "meant to be," they will find each other again. One wants freedom once the summer is over.

Themes: Relationships, love, choices, separation, control, selfishness

Actors: One guy and one girl

6.1L

Situation: Mr. Wrong comes home.

Conflict: Having just been released from prison, a guy goes back to his hometown to see his girlfriend, who hasn't had any communication with him since he was arrested. The girlfriend is shocked when she sees him; the boyfriend wants to pick up where they left off.

Spice it up: New boyfriend comes over in the middle of her conversation with the old boyfriend.

Themes: Regret, choices, consequences, differences

Actors: One guy and one girl (*Spice It Up:* One additional guy)

6.2
FAMILY CONFLICTS

6.2A

Situation: Mom and Dad are getting a divorce.

Conflict: Family of four is on vacation at Disney World when Mom and Dad decide they can't make their relationship work anymore. This trip was their last-ditch effort to "try." The kids react.

Spice It Up: Maybe a "character" from the theme park comes up right at an inopportune moment to get a "fun family photo." Does the brother take his aggression out on the character?

Themes: Divorce, words, consequences, adversity, crisis

Actors: One mom, one dad, and two kids (*Spice It Up:* One additional actor)

6.2B

Situation: Nurse, can you hold up my baby?

Conflict: Two proud dads are looking through the hospital nursery glass at their brand new babies and discussing what great dads they hope to be. As the conversation deepens, the two men express their fears and the regrets they have about their own fathers.

Spice It Up: One man's wife passed away while giving birth. How could God let this happen? Or one dad got his girlfriend pregnant; they're not married, and their future seems unstable already.

Themes: Parenthood, future, legacy, responsibility, fear

Actors: Two dads

6.2C

Situation: Grandma, can you hear me?

Conflict: Two siblings visit a grandparent in a nursing home. The grandparent doesn't respond to them at all. The siblings discuss how much they miss going to their grandparents' house and how much they dislike visiting the nursing home.

Spice It Up: After they exit, maybe the grandparent simply says quietly, "I love you." Or, toward the end, have the siblings freeze and let us hear the grandparent express: "If I could talk to you, I would say…"

Themes: Memories, relationships, family, love

Actors: Two siblings and one grandparent

6.2D

Situation: Gee, Mom! You're the best! Can I have some milk?

Conflict: A '50s TV show type of family is discussing how their days went. All is well until the youngest son enters with his new friend: a modern-day "Snoop Dogg" wannabe.

Spice It Up: Make the family modern and the friend a '50s TV show character.

Themes: Acceptance, differences, real (authenticity), values, culture, change

Actors: One mom, one dad, two siblings, and one "Snoop Dogg" friend

6.2E

Situation: Like father, like son

Conflict: Son who has not seen his father in years locates one of his father's old friends. The two have a conversation about why the son's dad left so long ago. The friend tries to guess what the dad must have been thinking and attempts to paint a good picture of him. The son expresses his pain of not having a dad through all these years.

Spice It Up: In the end, have the "friend" admit he's actually the son's long-lost father who gave him up for adoption long ago.

Themes: Anger, abandonment, relationships, understanding, adoption

Actors: One son and one older man

6.2F

Situation: I will ground you! I'm sorry, I didn't mean to hurt your self-esteem.

Conflict: Parents wait up for their teenager, who has stayed out too late with friends. Parents are afraid to discipline her because they don't want to hurt her self-esteem. As a result, the teenager runs all over the parents and knows the buttons to push to get out of punishment.

Spice It Up: Make the parents rednecks.

Themes: Respect, authority, rebellion, discipline, parenthood

Actors: One mom, one dad, and one son or daughter

6.2G

Situation: But Dear, he's just a child!

Conflict: Mom doesn't think child should get a summer job; Dad thinks the child needs to learn responsibility.

Themes: Responsibility, growing up, independence, maturity, work

Actors: One mom, one dad, and one son or daughter

6.2H

Situation: I forbid you to go out with…that person.

Conflict: Daughter tells her father that a boy she likes has finally asked her to the prom. Dad is all for it, until he learns her date is of a different ethnicity. Dad doesn't think he has any prejudices but is concerned about how others would perceive this type of date.

Themes: Dating, cultures, differences, values, respect, prejudice

Actors: One girl and one guy

6.2I

Situation: Don't go out in the deep end!

Conflict: Mom and son are at the swimming pool. Overly concerned mom gives constant warnings about the deep end: wearing floaties, watching out for earaches, applying sunscreen, etc. The problem is, the son is a teenager, and the overprotective mom has been doing this since he was little. The son decides to "cut the cord."

Themes: Independence, growing up, parenthood

Actors: One mom and one son

6.2J

Situation: I just want to see my dad!

Conflict: After a bitter divorce, Mom doesn't want her child to see her father. Dad has sent a letter to his daughter requesting a visit. She really wants to go, but Mom is against it. Daughter resents Mom for taking away the chance to know her father.

Spice It Up: Dad calls at the time the discussion is happening.

Themes: Divorce, regret, anger, control, spite (malice)

Actors: One mom and one son or daughter (*Spice It Up:* One dad on the phone)

6.2K

Situation: Monkey see, monkey do

Conflict: Older sibling approaches younger sibling to talk about some poor decisions he's making. In the conversation, the younger sibling admits he's just following the example that's been set for him by the older sibling.

Spice It Up: Have the conversation take place at the funeral of another sibling (or friend) who died because of making poor decisions.

Themes: Example, choices, influence, leadership, consequences

Actors: Two siblings

6.2L

Situation: It does make a difference; you're just the stepchild!

Conflict: Stepbrother and sister have an argument. It's obvious the stepsister is the "Golden Child." Stepbrother was used to having more freedom when it was just himself and his mom; he doesn't feel he's getting the respect he deserves from the stepsister or her dad. Mom wants the second marriage to work out and everyone to get along.

Spice it up: The two are the same age and go to school together. They hang out with two different crowds but are expected to come home, be nice to each other, and act like a "family."

Themes: Respect, values, divorce, compromise, family

Actors: One guy and one girl

6.3
WORK CONFLICTS

6.3A

Situation: Officer, you have the wrong person!

Conflict: Two police officers are sitting in a car outside a house on a stake-out, eating fast food, and having a discussion about what the "perpetrator" looks like. In the midst of their discussion, they get into either an argument or a deep debate about something that takes their eyes off of the house they should be watching. When a jogger comes by who matches a few of the characteristics of the criminal, the officers jump back to attention and arrest him, immune to his cries of innocence. No matter what the jogger does or says, the officers twist it since they already perceive him as the guilty party.

Spice It Up: Right after the arrest, the real perpetrator shows up with a gun and robs the police officers.

Themes: Focus, perception, innocence, guilt, hearing (listening), judgment

Actors: Two police officers and one jogger (Spice It Up: One additional actor)

6.3B

Situation: The catwalk tells the tale.

Conflict: The scene is a fashion show where the "models" are wearing clothes that express stereotypes of different teenagers: jock, geek, cheerleader, brain, etc. Two commentators point out their flaws as they walk the runway.

Spice It Up: Change the fashion show to one that expresses the feelings teenagers sometimes have about themselves: shame, guilt, inadequacy, depression, etc. In the end, let the "designer" come out to take a bow (the designer, of course, is Satan).

Themes: Feelings, cliques, stereotypes, self-esteem, judgment

Actors: Two commentators and as many models as you can find to represent the categories

6.3C

Situation: What's the biggie? We make chalk!

Conflict: Two workers who don't take their jobs seriously stand next to the conveyor belt at a chalk manufacturing line. Every so often the "chalk supervisor" comes in and reprimands them for not doing their job, giving them several reasons why they must pay attention and take pride in their work. The two workers don't see it that way.

Spice It Up: One worker thinks the chalk is just dust, and therefore, his job is insignificant, while the other worker believes the chalk to be an important tool for so many things. It turns out the chalk is used by construction crews to make sure everything fits together the way it should. We later hear that a new bridge falls during a heavy wind, killing 17 people, allegedly due to manufacturer defects.

Themes: Purpose, attitude, work, significance, faithfulness

Actors: Two workers and one supervisor

6.3D

Situation: Can I be as important as your job?

Conflict: Parent confronts teenage son about finding an illegal substance in his room. In the ensuing argument, the teenager expresses that the reason he experimented is because the parent is always at work.

Spice It Up: If drugs aren't a huge issue, then choose a more relevant topic for your group. Maybe the parent is mad because the teenager spends so much time playing video games, or at someone's house, or he doesn't try to spend "quality" time with the parents.

Themes: Work, priorities, parenthood, rebellion, addiction, neglect

Actors: One parent and one teenager

6.3E

Situation: Does this mean we're going to be homeless?

Conflict: Person tells another person she lost her job and doesn't know what to do. More importantly, she doesn't know how to feel about herself and why God would let this happen.

Spice It Up: A father must tell his family they have to cancel their highly anticipated vacation because he lost his job.

Themes: Disappointment, grief (loss), sovereignty of God

Actors: Two friends (*Spice It Up:* One dad and additional family members)

6.3F

Situation: Why do I have to wear this outfit again?

Conflict: Manager at a fast-food restaurant is training two new employees who quickly learn that the job includes not only a bizarre uniform, but also some bizarre ways of preparing food.

Spice It Up: The two new employees are best friends; one loves the bizarre stuff, and the other thinks it's weird. The restaurant manager is the father of one of them.

Themes: Humiliation, pride, responsibility, boundaries, safety

Actors: One manager and two new employees

6.3G

Situation: It's just an eraser...an ink pen...and a ream of paper.

Conflict: Worker confronts a coworker about stealing little things for personal use (e.g., paper clips, pens, markers, stamps, etc.).

Themes: Stealing, integrity, excuses, rationalization

Actors: Two coworkers

6.3H

Situation: This is the "better life" you were talking about?

Conflict: Mom comes home from work late to find her daughter has been waiting up so she can tell her the good news: She has made the volleyball team. Since Dad passed away, Mom has sought to create a better life, taking a new job that has brought more money but longer hours at the office. Daughter is feeling left out of Mom's new way of life.

Spice it up: First volleyball match is same time Mom is supposed to attend a conference for work in a different state.

Themes: Loss, grief, quality time, money, love, change, sacrifices, neglect, loneliness

Actors: One mom and one daughter

6.3I

Situation: Hey buddy…you're fired.

Conflict: Boss tells a shift supervisor to fire an employee who happens to be the shift supervisor's best friend. Even though he helped him get hired, the shift supervisor has to tell his best friend he's fired and the reasons why. Shift supervisor knows his friend will get defensive and blame everyone except himself.

Themes: Honesty, responsibility, attitude, blame, integrity

Actors: One boss, one shift supervisor, and one employee

6.3J

Situation: There's a fly in my soup!

Conflict: Customer is slurping down his favorite soup and suddenly realizes he's eaten a huge fly. Customer is outraged and calls the server over to complain about the fly. Thinking the customer only wants a free meal, the server doesn't believe the customer.

Spice it Up: The manager of the restaurant comes by to see what the commotion is all about. Have another actor find something else in her food.

Themes: Anger, image, persuasion, service, perception

Actors: One server and one customer (*Spice It Up:* One manager and an additional customer)

6.3K

Situation: Hey boss, here's the deal: I've got a deadly virus.

Conflict: Girlfriend or buddy drops two concert tickets in Actor 1's lap. Actor 1 wants to go but is scheduled to work that night. He calls his boss to explain that he has gotten really sick. Boss thinks Actor 1 is lying and asks for him to put a parent on the phone. Buddy or girlfriend takes the call and acts like Mom or Dad.

Spice It Up: On his way home from work, the boss stops by with chicken soup, hoping Actor 1 is feeling better.

Themes: Honesty, responsibility, choices, consequences

Actors: Two guys or one guy and one girl, and one boss (*Spice It Up:* One mom or one dad)

6.3L

Situation: Where did you get all those Benjamins?

Conflict: Actor 1 confronts Actor 2 about all the money Actor 2 has seemed to acquire from her job. Both are employed at the same place; however, Actor 1 works many more hours than Actor 2. Actor 1 has evidence that Actor 2 has been cheating on her timecard.

Spice It Up: Boss awards Actor 2 "Employee of the Month" for all of the long hours worked.

Themes: Confrontation, work, cheating, lies, character, jealousy, lying (honesty)

Actors: Two employees (*Spice It Up:* One boss)

6.4

BELIEVER/SEEKER CONFLICTS

6.4A

Situation: You and God used to be so tight.

Conflict: Actor 1 decided to follow Christ after hanging around Actor 2. Over the past year, Actor 2 has completely changed his attitudes and behavior; he has given up on God and doesn't believe the whole "salvation" thing anymore. Actor 1 wants to know why and confronts his friend and spiritual mentor about why he walked away from God.

Themes: Doubt (confusion), crisis, belief

Actors: Two friends

6.4B

Situation: This is how you represent?

Conflict: On the last night of camp, a few campers share about what God has done in their hearts over the past week. Another person stands up to talk and tells the group she doesn't believe in God but was open to see how Christians lived and what they believed. After spending a week with them, she has decided that Christianity is not for her because the actions and the words she witnessed during the week didn't match up to what was being said on the last night of camp.

Spice It Up: A believer stands up after the last person's condemnation to confess and ask for another chance to show what a real Christian is like.

Themes: Arrogance, hypocrisy, witnessing (evangelism), actions, disappointment

Actors: Three or four believers who share and one seeker who shares (Spice It Up: One additional believer who asks forgiveness for actions)

6.4C

Situation: Conversation from the afterlife

Conflict: Three friends are sitting together, talking about someone who passed away, and wondering about the state of their friend's soul. When the third person talks, the other two don't seem to respond to anything he says. As the skit continues, you realize the third friend is the one who died and is trying to tell them what has happened to him.

Spice It Up: The third friend committed suicide and wonders why the other two friends didn't express their feelings before his death.

Themes: Death, suicide, memories, judgment, evangelism, friendship

Actors: Three friends

6.4D

Situation: Back from heaven, I see.

Conflict: Actors 1 and 2 used to be best friends until one became a Christian and the other didn't. After Actor 1 became a Christian, she left her old friends and started hanging out with the "church crowd." Actor 2 never understood why she was suddenly given the heave-ho. When they finally get an opportunity to talk, will Actor 1 clam up or talk about her newfound faith? Will Actor 2 be receptive or just feel rejected?

Themes: Rejection, salvation, evangelism, friendship, love

Actors: Two friends

6.4E

Situation: By the way, did anyone tell him about the love of God?

Conflict: Some friends gather back at their hometown for a former classmate's funeral. One by one, they share a memory of their deceased friend. As three or four people share about the "good times," the last actor starts to tell about something but can't finish because he suddenly realizes they never had a conversation about Christ. Did anyone share with this person about the love of God? No one can answer the question.

Themes: Evangelism, death, eternity, friendship

Actors: Four or five mourners at a funeral

6.4F

Situation: I give up!

Conflict: Actors 1 and 2 have been praying for Actor 3 since they were all in middle school. Every time the three of them talk, the conversation always veers toward religion, and more questions are brought up than answers. Actor 3 doesn't really like to hang around with them anymore. Actor 1 is fed up and wants to give up on Actor 3—no more praying for him, no more trying. Actor 2 sees it a little differently, even though it seems like there hasn't been much fruit and God doesn't seem to be answering them in this matter.

Spice It Up: Actor 3 knocks on their dorm room door to talk.

Themes: Prayer, responsibility, compassion, perseverance, faith

Actors: Two friends (*Spice It Up:* One additional friend)

6.4G

Situation: See, Mom, it's like this…

Conflict: Daughter has just come home from church. Not only are her parents not believers, but they also don't approve of—and are very vocal about—the recent change in their child. They don't like organized religion, and they don't believe Jesus was the Son of God. Every time she comes home from church, she faces the heartache of getting the third degree about why she believes this "brainwashed nonsense."

Themes: Atheism (unbelief), example, parenthood, love, patience

Actors: One mom, one dad, and one son or daughter

6.4H

Situation: Still crazy after all these years

Conflict: Young adult runs into his old college girlfriend. He tries to explain what he has been up to lately, and the ex-girlfriend doesn't buy the fact that he has found God because of the lifestyle he lived back in the "good old days." The ex knows all about the old lifestyle and the things they did together. No matter how hard he tries to explain his change of heart, the ex still finds it all laughable.

Themes: Sin, condemnation, discouragement, consequences, choices, friendship

Actors: One guy and one girl

6.4I

Situation: Have no fear—Super Christian is here!

Conflict: Super Christian and his sidekick, Bible Boy, talk to their TV audience about evangelism; the two encourage their viewers to go out and share the gospel with the "Lost Leroys" and "Wandering Wandas" at their schools. Bible Boy warns the boys and girls to watch out for the "Hateful Harrys" and the "Carrie Cults" of the world. The duo acts out different scenarios their audience might come across in the world to help out the boys and girls in TV Land.

Themes: Evangelism, testimony, encouragement, authenticity

Actors: Two actors

6.4J

Situation: That homeless person is making way too much noise.

Conflict: On a beautiful Saturday afternoon, a homeless person claiming to be a prophet stands in the middle of the park preaching repentance to anyone who can hear him. Two or three other sets of actors pass by to put in their two cents about Jesus and ask why he insists on preaching when no one cares to listen.

Themes: Truth, evangelism, rejection, perseverance, faith

Actors: One homeless man and three to five passers-by

6.4K

Situation: Hello, caller, you are on the air.

Conflict: Announcer at a local talk radio station is taking calls on the subject of "something to believe in." People of all different backgrounds call in (from offstage) to say what they believe in.

Spice It Up: One caller says she is truly looking for the meaning of life, but it seems like no one is really living what they believe.

Themes: Searching, belief, purpose, differences

Actors: One host and five or six callers (Feel free to use characters from section 7.2.) (*Spice It Up:* One additional caller who is searching for purpose)

6.4L

Situation: I want what you have.

Conflict: Actor 1 has been a Christian for quite some time and has always demonstrated the love of God through his actions. However, recently, he has strayed away and is at the point where he is considering throwing it all away for what the world has to offer. Out of touch since high school, Actor 2 remembers Actor 1 as a person who wasn't afraid to live for God and tracks him down to ask how to have what Actor 1 has.

Themes: Witness (evangelism), faithfulness, guilt (innocence), giving up, influence, choices, redemption, forgiveness

Actors: Two actors

6.5
SCHOOL CONFLICTS

6.5A

Situation: Let's go out and win one for the Dipper!

Conflict: Have your audience be a team that's getting ready for the big game—but the catch is, the coach can't seem to remember some very important things (e.g., players' names, team mascot, what sport they play, the rules to the sport, etc.). In the background, two assistant coaches gently try to keep the coach on track while remaining supportive.

Themes: Leadership, forgetfulness, teamwork, support, competition

Actors: One head coach and two assistant coaches

6.5B

Situation: Slide your paper on over…

Conflict: During class, Actor 1 wants to cheat from Actor 2's paper. Actor 3 overhears everything and wonders whether she should keep her mouth shut or say something.

Spice It Up: Introduce the teacher into the mix. She knows someone is cheating, and unless someone "spills the beans," she's going give everyone in the class a failing grade.

Themes: Honesty, integrity, cheating, peer-pressure, consequences

Actors: Three students (*Spice It Up:* One teacher)

6.5C

Situation: I heard the biggest rumor!

Conflict: Two friends (Actors 1 and 2) come up to the third friend (Actor 3) in the hallway at school and begin to tell him about a "nasty rumor"

floating around. While Actors 1 and 2 can't figure out whom the rumor is about, Actor 3 is taken aback because it sounds like something that happened to him over the weekend; however, the story has gotten totally out of control. Actor 3 begins to set the record straight about what really happened.

Spice It Up: The "rumor" turns out to be true. How does Actor 3 respond now that everyone knows?

Themes: Rumors, words, friendships, gossip, truth, responsibility

Actors: Three friends

6.5D

Situation: The principal is our "pal."

Conflict: Student has been called into the principal's office. Although the student thinks she's been called in for doing something terrible, the principal actually wants to inform the student that she's been recommended for a "Student of the Year" award. Before the principal can tell the student about the honor, she starts confessing all the things she has done at and to the school throughout the year.

Themes: Conscience, confessions, perceptions, guilt (innocence), misunderstandings

Actors: One principal and one student

6.5E

Situation: Lunch Lady Land

Conflict: A couple of lunch ladies are having a conversation with a couple of school custodians. Their discussion ranges from what's really in the chef's special to the proper way to clean a toilet, from how overlooked they are by the students to how much they believe in the students.

Spice It Up: Have a couple of students walk by and make fun of the lunch ladies and custodians.

Themes: Respect, service, recognition, arrogance

Actors: Two lunch ladies and one or two custodians (*Spice It Up:* Two students)

6.5F

Situation: I know what you did last summer.

Conflict: In class, students are giving speeches about what they did over the summer break. The stories range from boring to fascinating. The last classmate tells how he went on a mission trip and helped people in need.

Spice It Up: Have some people make fun of the last student for "wasting his summer."

Themes: Mission trip, witnessing (evangelism), compassion, motives, values

Actors: Three to five classmates

6.5G

Situation: Romeo, Romeo…line, please.

Conflict: Drama department is putting on a production of *Romeo and Juliet.* The only problem is, Romeo has forgotten his lines and is making up his dialogue, hoping no one will notice. Juliet catches on quickly and begins to lose her cool.

Spice it Up: Throw in different characters to try to get Romeo back on his lines.

Themes: Anger, forgetfulness, discipline, patience, responsibility

Actors: One guy and one girl (*Spice It Up:* One or two additional actors)

6.5H

Situation: The word is "plenipotentiary."

Conflict: Tension mounts as the final three contestants compete in the middle school spelling bee. How do the contestants behave when they are under pressure for the grand prize?

Spice It Up: The words given by the spelling bee administrator are really simple, but the final three are wound so tightly that they can't figure out how to spell them.

Themes: Performance, competition, stress, anxiety (fear)

Actors: Three classmates and one administrator

6.5I

Situation: If I'm elected class president…

Conflict: Position of student body president is up for grabs as four classmates try to win the audience over by telling how they would run the school if elected.

Spice It Up: Pick different characters from section 7.2 and assign them to the nominees before they make their speeches.

Themes: Influence, promises, persuasion, dignity, leadership, pride, ambition

Actors: Four classmates

6.5J

Situation: Seat's taken; can't sit here.

Conflict: Actor 1 is trying to find a seat in the lunchroom. She goes to sit down with Actors 2 and 3, whom she thinks are friends. Actors 2 and 3 begin to come up with different reasons why Actor 1 cannot sit with them.

Themes: Rejection, peer pressure, excuses, humiliation, acceptance, cruelty

Actors: Three classmates

6.5K

Situation: Bell rang…time for recess!

Conflict: Group of first graders is outside during recess. Each kid tells what she wants to be when she grows up. As each classmate explains what she would like to be, the others think it's not a very good option and come up with a better idea. (Keep in mind they are seven years old.)

Spice It Up: Fast-forward to their 20-year class reunion. How did their lives turn out?

Themes: Legacy, dreams, goals, maturity, faith, ambition

Actors: Five or six schoolmates

6.5L

Situation: Please welcome your valedictorian…

Conflict: Class valedictorian begins a typical graduation speech. The actor stops after reading the first few, obviously scripted lines, gets rid of his notes, and begins to get real with his audience. The actor begins to talk about what he witnessed and experienced during the past four years of high school: peer pressure, cliques, conformity, exclusiveness, etc., and asks: What kinds of people will they become in the future?

Theme: Peer pressure, cliques, regrets, opportunity

Actors: One valedictorian

6.6
FRIENDSHIP CONFLICTS

6.6A

Situation: With friends like these...

Conflict: Two women are getting their nails done at a salon. The two women are sitting back-to-back, each one facing the person doing her nails. They take turns talking to the person doing their nails about their "supposed" best friend, including why that person is a lousy friend. They begin to overhear each other's conversation and agree with what's being said. In the end, the two women turn around and see that they are talking about each other.

Themes: Gossip, bitterness, hearing (listening), friendship, forgiveness, loyalty

Actors: Two girlfriends and two nail manicurists

6.6B

Situation: Brother, can you spare a dime?

Conflict: Two friends are shopping together. Actor 1 has just enough money to buy lunch and the new CD he's been saving for. Actor 2 spent his money on something else and subsequently doesn't have any money to buy lunch. Does Actor 1 loan Actor 2 money and put off getting the new CD?

Themes: Money, priorities, discipline, generosity, sharing (greed)

Actors: Two guys or two girls

6.6C

Situation: We're just friends.

Conflict: Actor 1 has discovered that Actor 2 has been talking on the phone a little too much to Actor 1's girlfriend or boyfriend. Actor 1 decides to confront Actor 2.

Spice It Up: Actor 2 knows the girlfriend or boyfriend is going to break up with Actor 1 but has been sworn to secrecy.

Themes: Honesty, secrets, betrayal, boundaries, friendships

Actors: Two guys or two girls

6.6D

Situation: Whose side are you on?

Conflict: Three friends discuss what they're going to do for the evening. One wants to go to the movies, and another wants to go bowling. Each tries to convince the third friend to join her side.

Spice It Up: Instead of the movies or bowling, the friends want to do things they shouldn't. The third friend is a Christian who has a tough time deciding what to do.

Themes: Choices, influence, convictions, compromise

Actors: Three friends

6.6E

Situation: April Fools!

Conflict: Small group of friends is hanging out together. In the process of talking, some of the friends start playing jokes on the others. Though they start out innocently, the jokes gradually become mean.

Spice It Up: Someone is actually serious, and the others think he's joking.

Themes: Discernment, trust, hurt, boundaries, compassion, malice

Actors: Four or five guys and girls

6.6F

Situation: I just want to be loved—is that so wrong?

Conflict: Actor 1 desperately tries to fit into the "popular group." She feels that if she can fit in with them, then she will be "somebody." But despite her feeble attempts at looking the part, the popular group doesn't warm up to her. She only succeeds in annoying the group and becoming a target for their cruelty.

Spice It Up: After Actor 1 is humiliated, a true friend comes across her path.

Themes: Acceptance, significance, popularity, inner worth, self-esteem

Actors: One actor and three or four "popular people" (*Spice It Up:* One "real friend")

6.6G

Situation: You're my "backup" friend.

Conflict: Actor 1 realizes Actor 2 is no friend at all. Actor 2 is nice to Actor 1's face and wants to hang out with him when no one "cooler" is available. Actor 1 is tired of being a doormat and confronts Actor 2 on his behavior. Actor 2 takes offense and tries to convince Actor 1 it's all in his head.

Spice It Up: Have a "cooler" person come into the scene to show Actor 2's true colors.

Themes: Friendship, dignity, inner worth

Actors: Two friends (*Spice It Up:* One "cooler" person)

6.6H

Situation: When did that person become your new best friend?

Conflict: Actor 1 is feeling jealous over Actor 2's new friend. Actor 2 has been spending a lot of time with a classmate who's older and has a car. Feeling rejected, Actor 1 decides to see what's so great about this new best friend; he goes over to Actor 2's house, where Actor 2 and his new friend are laughing and having a great time. What happens next?

Themes: Rejection, loneliness, loyalty, jealousy, materialism, selfishness

Actors: Two friends and one new friend

6.6I

Situation: Goodbye, my dear, college is here.

Conflict: Group of best friends, who has been with each other since grade school, has a final get-together before they go off to different colleges, states, jobs, etc. What do these goodbyes look like? How do the actors show the history of their friendships and the humor and heartache of a fond farewell?

Spice It Up: One friend tells another she has had a crush on him since they were little kids.

Themes: Relationships, memories, maturity, the future

Actors: Four or five guys and girls

6.6J

Situation: The ultimate sleepover

Conflict: Group of friends stays up late talking about the serious aspects of their friendships. It seems like some things haven't been talked about for a very long time.

Themes: Honesty, confession, relationships, forgiveness

Actors: Three or four friends

6.6K

Situation: There's something I haven't told you.

Conflict: Actor 1 confesses an issue to Actor 2. The particular issue involves dishonesty with Actor 2 that's been going on for quite a while. Will Actor 2 forgive Actor 1? Actor 1 tries to make amends, but it may be too little, too late, since a good part of their friendship has been built on a lie.

Themes: Anger, forgiveness, humility, honesty (lying), confession

Actors: Two friends

6.6L

Situation: You are my best friend.

Conflict: Girl and guy have been best friends since grade school. They've always been there for one another and have always had an attraction to each other, but they never dated, because they were afraid of ruining the friendship. The two are now in college and decide to talk about the possibility of being more than best friends. One thinks they should stay friends; the other wants to pursue a romantic relationship.

Spice It Up: One of the actors has a date that night; the other one shows up at the friend's dorm room unannounced.

Themes: True love, friendship, dating, risk, vulnerability

Actors: One guy and one girl (*Spice It Up:* One date)

6.7
TABOO CONFLICTS

6.7A

Situation: Hi, I'm Miguel, your barista.

Conflict: Two students are in a coffee shop. The person working at the counter is from a different country, and the students have a difficult time understanding him. The students begin to make fun of the coffee shop worker.

Spice It Up: The coffee shop worker comes over to the two students and tells them he visited their church last week.

Themes: Prejudice, malice, differences, hypocrisy

Actors: Two students and one barista

6.7B

Situation: What do you mean, you "have to get out of here"?

Conflict: Two friends are hanging out. At some point, Actor 1 says, "I've got to get out of here." Actor 2 agrees and says she has to go, also. There's a little confusion, until Actor 1 says, "You don't understand, I've got to go…I've got to get out of my house and go somewhere else." As the improv continues, Actor 1 divulges that something has gone terribly wrong at home and she has to get out of there. Have the issue be abuse of some kind. How can the friend help? Is there any advice she can offer?

Themes: Abuse, honesty, friendship, secrets, trust

Actors: Two friends

6.7C

Situation: How did those pop-ups get on my computer?

Conflict: Mom finds pornography on the family computer and confronts her teenage son about it. The student tries to come up with as many excuses as possible, but the longer he talks, the more ridiculous and guilty he sounds.

Spice It Up: Dad enters the room. After a little discussion, he confesses that the porn is his.

Themes: Internet, pornography, purity (holiness), confession, consequences, confrontation, honesty

Actors: One mom and one son (*Spice It Up:* One dad)

6.7D

Situation: What do you see in him?

Conflict: It's a girl's first date, and her family is so excited. Everyone is smiling, until the doorbell rings and her date is obviously from a very poor family. Although he doesn't have a lot of money or the perfect manners, he has a lot of heart, and the girl sees something in him the parents are not willing to see for fear of what the "neighborhood" or "country club" friends will think once word gets out about with whom their daughter went to the dance.

Themes: Money, dating, prejudice, image, values, inner worth

Actors: One mom, one dad, one daughter, and one date

6.7E

Situation: You want that other chicken leg?

Conflict: Group of friends is sharing a meal together. Everyone seems to notice how one skinny girl is putting away the food. They start to bug her about how she can eat so much and stay so skinny. In the discussion, she reveals she is bulimic.

Spice It Up: Maybe the girl who struggles with bulimia knows things about some of the other friends and, in defense, starts spilling the beans on their struggles.

Themes: Eating disorders, honesty, secrets, vulnerability, self-esteem

Actors: One girl and two or three friends

6.7F

Situation: I'm such a better warrior than you.

Conflict: Group of friends is playing a violent video game. While playing, they discuss whether video games lead to violence and finally decide such theories are wrong.

However, as the improv goes on, they all seem to get more intense and physical.

Spice It Up: Instead of a violent video game, the only game they can get to work is one of their little sister's *Barbie's Swan Lake* video games.

Themes: Violence, influence, competition, rage (anger)

Actors: Three or four guys

6.7G

Situation: We need to have "the talk."

Conflict: Mom or Dad sits down with a child of the same gender to talk about sex. Mom or Dad feels the child must know about "the birds and the bees" before he or she begins high school. Kid doesn't really want to have the talk with the parent.

Spice it Up: Single parent has to give the talk to a child of the opposite sex. Child knows more about sex than parent was aware of.

Themes: Sex, knowledge, boundaries, communication

Actors: One parent and one child

6.7H

Situation: What makes him that way?

Conflict: School friends start making fun of another classmate (Actor 1), because they think he acts like he's a homosexual. Actor 1 overhears the teasing and confronts his classmates about their attitudes toward and treatment of him.

Spice it Up: Actor 1 tells them he *is* gay. The other classmates are shocked. A discussion follows.

Themes: Homosexuality, truth, acceptance, understanding, loneliness, cruelty

Actors: One actor and two or three classmates

6.7I

Situation: I cut myself to feel.

Conflict: Actors 1 and 2 are walking home from school when Actor 1 sees cut marks on Actor 2's wrists and arms. Actor 2 does her best to hide them and make excuses but realizes she's been found out. Actor 1 doesn't understand why Actor 2 would hurt herself in this way. Actor 2 can explain the cutting in one of two ways: to be able to feel something in a life bound by numbness, or to cover up unbearable pain from a certain situation in her life.

Themes: Self-mutilation, hurt, healing, hiding, pain

Actors: Two girls

6.7J

Situation: I feel like I carry around this 10-pound weight.

Conflict: Actor 1 has been molested as a child. While he cannot remember many of the details of the abuse or the identity of the perpetrator, a lack of trust always seems to be undermining his relationships. Two of his friends come to talk to Actor 1 about why he seems to sabotage their friendships. Actor 1 doesn't want to be vulnerable but must extend a little truth so his friends will understand. Both friends decide not to give up on Actor 1.

Themes: Trust, hurt, abuse, healing, freedom

Actors: Three friends

6.7K

Situation: Let's hear your side.

Conflict: Teams from two schools debate the topic of euthanasia: Is it *murder*, or is it *mercy*? Two people on each side of the debate give their perspectives on the issue.

Spice It Up: Let the audience vote right after the debate on whether they have been influenced for or against euthanasia.

Themes: Euthanasia, murder, mercy (compassion), suffering

Actors: Four debate members

6.7L

Situation: You're what?

Conflict: Girlfriend tells boyfriend she's pregnant. She took two tests, and both came back positive—so there's no doubt about it. One wants to get married and do the "right thing." The other wants to talk seriously about having an abortion, not only because a baby will mess up their plans for the future, but also because neither of them are ready to be parents and it'll be in the best long-term interests of the child.

Themes: Abortion, pre-marital sex, marriage, choices, consequences

Actors: One guy and one girl

6.8

FAITH CONFLICTS

6.8A

Situation: Let us worship.

Conflict: Group of actors presents a regular worship service, but instead of actually talking or singing, all they can say is, "Blah, blah, blah." (Be sure to have them imitate the ministers at your church while they do this.)

Spice It Up: As the service goes on, an actor planted in the audience stands up to express that she is looking for something more than just the same old Sunday morning routine.

Themes: Worship, routine, tradition, searching

Actors: A mix of four or five girls and guys

6.8B

Situation: What's the deal with the fat guy?

Conflict: Group of friends is waiting to be seated at a popular Chinese restaurant. As they pass the time, someone asks a question about the big Buddha statue and what that religion is all about. The following discussion shows how much they know or don't know about the religion.

Spice It Up: Choose a different type of location that would lend itself to discussing a different religion.

Themes: Religions, beliefs, knowledge, searching

Actors: A mix of three to five girls and guys

6.8C

Situation: Just answer the question, sir.

Conflict: Actor 1 is on trial for being a Christian. A variety of witnesses is brought in to prove or disprove the case.

Spice It Up: Choose up to 12 audience members to be a jury who will give a verdict at the end of the trial. Add some lawyers to cross-examine Actor 1.

Themes: Actions, lifestyle, example, accountability, testimony

Actors: One actor and several witnesses (*Spice It Up:* Up to 12 jury members and one or two lawyers)

6.8D

Situation: I got my test results back…

Conflict: Small group from a church is meeting together when one member gets a phone call. The doctor's office has called to report that the biopsy they took last week came back as a malignant cancer. The ensuing conversation reveals different levels of faith in the group.

Themes: Support, prayer, fear, death, hope, crisis, provision of God

Actors: One person who is diagnosed and two or three friends

6.8E

Situation: I always feel like somebody's watching me.

Conflict: Actor 1 tries to tell Actor 2 why it's so hard to move ahead in her relationship with God. Actor 1 feels dejected, unable to shed the guilt and shame of her past choices and actions. She is convinced that God will never be able to change or use her. Actor 2 talks to Actor 1 about what she believes about God's forgiveness, as well as how most of the heroes of the Bible had pretty terrible pasts, too.

Spice it up: Add three or four "ghosts" who talk into Actor 1's ear (representing different "sins" from her past). Only Actor 1 can hear the ghosts.

Themes: Regret, lying (dishonesty), deception, inner worth, forgiveness, holiness, redemption, freedom

Actors: Two friends (*Spice It Up:* Three or four "ghosts" from Actor 1's past)

6.8F

Situation: Thy word is a lamp unto my…my…I forgot.

Conflict: During a church service, the pastor calls on people to give testimonies of how memorizing Scripture has helped them. The pastor chooses three people who quote a verse of Scripture from memory and give a reason why this helped them in a particular situation. The fourth person the pastor calls on admits, after fumbling through a verse, that he hasn't memorized any Scripture since he became a believer almost 10 years ago.

Themes: Bible (Word of God), testimony, dedication, faithfulness, obedience

Actors: One pastor, three congregants, and one congregant who hasn't memorized anything

6.8G

Situation: The waiting room

Conflict: Brother waits for younger sister to arrive at the hospital where he must tell her the bad news: Dad's cancer is back. Brother knows his sister's faith isn't as strong as it used to be; her heart has grown callous, bitter, and cynical toward God. Brother tries talking to his sister about faith and how relying on it is now more important than ever.

Themes: Crisis, family, pain, bitterness, hope

Actors: One big brother and one sister

6.8H

Situation: I wish I could go home.

Conflict: Convinced God has called him to the mission field, Actor 1 goes on a two-week mission trip. One particular day, a group of soldiers carrying automatic weapons confronts Actor 1 and one other missionary; the soldiers want to know why the missionaries are on their land, how many more are with them, and what the books are that they keep giving to the indigenous people. It's a life-or-death situation like they've never known before. Do the two missionaries tell the soldiers everything, or do they walk away without mentioning the God they serve?

Themes: Belief, missionaries, evangelism, courage, faith

Actors: Two missionaries and three or four soldiers

6.8I

Situation: Great sermon this morning; please pass the salsa.

Conflict: After church, a group of friends has lunch together at a local restaurant. They discuss the sermon about faith that the pastor gave that morning; then the conversation turns to their own personal problems that never seem to get resolved.

Themes: Pessimism, unhappiness, selfishness, Word of God, testimony

Actors: A mix of three or four guys and girls

6.8J

Situation: Just one of those days

Conflict: Actor 1 has a talk with God after a rotten day. She has just received a rejection letter from the only college she applied to. Most of her friends will be going to this school, but she'll be stuck at a local community college. Feeling like this will sabotage her future and disappoint her parents, the girl's faith is tested. How does she react to God and to life?

Spice it up: Offstage and unseen, an actor playing the voice of God responds to the girl's questions.

Themes: Hardship (adversity), prayer, disappointment, sovereignty of God, crisis

Actors: One actor (*Spice It Up:* One additional actor for voice of God)

6.8K

Situation: I know it's late; are you still online?

Conflict: Actor 1 has been trying to find the right time to start a conversation with Actor 2 via Instant Messenger. Actor 2 has fallen away from God and sees no reason to fully commit his life to Christ when there are so many things to explore and do before he dies. He believes sin is just a word church people use to promote fear. Actor 1 talks to Actor 2 about his faith and his concern that Actor 2's choices are going to lead to some hurtful consequences.

(Keep in mind: If you do this with computers, actors have to pretend to be typing, never look at one another, and still talk while they pretend to type.)

Themes: Grace, truth, pride, conviction, evangelism, encouragement

Actors: Two friends

6.8L

Situation: God, where's the deliverance?

Conflict: Wife is just about to give up praying for a certain circumstance. She has been asking God for years that this request would be answered, but after five years, she sees no change, and strong doubt has set in. Her spouse tries to encourage her to keep the faith that answers will come, even though both are frustrated and weary.

Themes: Dreams, doubt, sadness (grief), prayer, encouragement

Actors: One husband and one wife

6.9
SIN CONFLICTS

6.9A

Situation: I'm sorry, I wasn't thinking.

Conflict: Actor 1 finds out Actor 2 has brought something on a church trip that isn't allowed, such as cigarettes or Tarot cards. Actor 2 tries to play it down. Actor 1 has to decide what to do about her discovery.

Spice It Up: Make it something like alcohol or drugs that was brought on the trip.

Themes: Accountability, choices, conscience, mistakes, denial

Actors: Two friends

6.9B

Situation: I'm bored. Let's do something stupid.

Conflict: Group of friends is sitting around with nothing to do. As they discuss their different options, ideas begin to turn toward things they shouldn't do. Finally they decide on something; however, one member of the group isn't willing to go along.

Themes: Choices, influence, boredom, purpose, peer pressure

Actors: A mix of three to five girls and guys

6.9C

Situation: Who are you really?

Conflict: Actor 1 is stressed out when his two worlds collide. His double life is revealed when someone from his church meets someone he parties with on the weekends.

Themes: Integrity, partying, authenticity, testimony

Actors: Three actors

6.9D

Situation: We're just like you.

Conflict: Actor 1 has agreed to meet with Actors 2 and 3 to discuss possibly joining their religion. Actor 1 soon realizes the religion is a cult.

Spice It Up: Make a serious subject more lighthearted by making the cult do really bizarre and silly things.

Themes: Cults, religions, beliefs, truth, discernment, knowledge

Actors: Three actors

6.9E

Situation: I didn't do anything.

Conflict: Two friends are finishing their regular accountability meeting by offering encouragements to each other about how well they seem to be doing. Actor 1 asks Actor 2 to use her phone. A sexually suggestive text message comes in at the same time she is about to dial. Actor 1 accesses Actor 2's recent text messages and realizes their accountability time has been more of a show than truly wanting to stay pure before God.

Themes: Accountability, deeds (actions), responsibility, deception, addiction, secrets

Actors: Two guys or two girls

6.9F

Situation: It's no big deal…everyone does it.

Conflict: Parent confronts child about finding a stolen pad of hall passes from the school. The child feels like it's no big deal, because everyone else he knows does it.

Spice It Up: Maybe instead of a pad of hall passes, the parent discovers his teen has been letting his friends sneak into the movie theater where he works.

Themes: Stealing, lifestyle, actions, rationalizing, peer pressure

Actors: One parent and one teenager

6.9G

Situation: It's okay; we're all Christians.

Conflict: Group of friends lives in the "gray area" on a certain sin they have rationalized to the point where they feel it's "okay." Though they're able to make room for their own choices, the group passes judgment on other Christians who sin or make mistakes.

Spice It Up: A member of the youth group approaches the group and graciously speaks the truth about the group's actions and behavior regarding the gray area.

Themes: Rationalization, lifestyle, complacency, convictions, condemnation

Actors: Three or four friends (*Spice It Up:* One truth teller from their youth group)

6.9H

Situation: Let's go to a different church.

Conflict: Several friends who are regular attendees of the youth group tell their youth pastor they're going to find a different church because they "just aren't getting fed" and have outgrown the programs. They compare their youth group to what some of the other churches are doing and how many students they have.

Spice It Up: The youth minister or leader tells them to go ahead and find another church.

Themes: Idols, pride, image, selfishness

Actors: Two or three friends (*Spice It Up:* One youth minister or leader)

6.9I

Situation: What you are experiencing is an intervention.

Conflict: Group of friends holds an intervention for a friend who has become too deeply involved in an "Internet romance" and has decided she wants to meet the person on the other side of the screen. The friends step in to try to tell her how dangerous the outcome could be.

Spice It Up: The girlfriends have discovered the identity of the so-called "love interest," who is 10 years older than he said he was. Does this dissuade their love-hungry friend?

Themes: Internet, deception, hope, support, risks

Actors: One friend and two or three friends doing the intervention

6.9J

Situation: Money changes everything.

Conflict: Two childhood friends cross paths at the mall. The two had been the closest of friends, until Actor 1's father made a great deal of money in his business and moved his family into the wealthiest neighborhood in town. As they talk, the two realize how different they have become. Actor 1's values are tainted by snobbery and greed; Actor 2 envies Actor 1's easy life.

Spice It Up: Actor 2's dad has just lost his job from Actor 1's dad's company

Themes: Money, differences, change, envy (jealousy), greed, materialism

Actors: Two friends

6.9K

Situation: I can eat you under the table.

Conflict: Group of buddies gathers around the big screen for the big game. As they watch the game, they cram pretzels, hot dogs, cookies, soft drinks, etc., into their mouths without thinking of the consequences. The more they eat, the more miserable they become, but they ignore their bodies and keep indulging.

Spice It Up: The guys decide to have a competition of their own that involves eating, drinking, and physical challenges. The first one to vomit loses.

Themes: Excess, self-control, indulgence, consequences, competition

Actors: Four or five guys

6.9L

Situation: Pride is something you trip over.

Conflict: Manager speaks with an employee regarding a series of mistakes on her shift. Employee doesn't see any of the issues the manager brings up as her fault but instead blames everyone else she can think of. The employee spends most of the confrontation blind to her own faults, defending her actions, and leaving the manager with no choice but termination.

Spice It Up: Manager brings in another person who has witnessed incidents of the employee's poor job performance.

Themes: Pride, confrontation, excuses, responsibility, blame, denial

Actors: One manager and one employee (*Spice It Up:* One additional employee giving account)

6.10
JUST FOR FUN CONFLICTS

6.10A

Situation: It's a dog-day afternoon.

Conflict: Two actors play dogs being taken to a dog park by their human owners. The dogs discuss their lives. The owners also discuss their lifestyle (which is completely different than their faithful friends).

Spice It Up: Let the dogs talk and have the humans say, "Blah, blah, blah," instead of actually talking. Introduce a cat into the mix and see what happens.

Themes: Family, lifestyles, differences, discernment, perception

Actors: Two dogs and two owners (Spice It Up: One cat)

6.10B

Situation: Do as I say, not as I do…

Conflict: Tour guide explains to her tour group that their visit to the old land-mine field should be safe as long as everyone does exactly what the tour guide does. All is fine until the tour guide swallows a fly. As she goes "crazy" trying to shake and cough up the fly, the people in the tour group imitate her every action.

Spice It Up: Have the guide step on a mine and realize that if she moves, it will blow up. The skit can take a more serious note as the guide discusses what she has done with her life.

Themes: Example, leadership, discernment, choices, influence

Actors: One tour guide, no more than four people in the group

6.10C

Situation: Did someone just pass gas in here?

Conflict: Small group of people is riding in an elevator together. Each of them has his own quirk (picking nose, clearing throat, thinking people are looking at him, etc.).

Spice It Up: The elevator gets stuck.

Themes: Differences, acceptance, habits, stereotypes, teamwork

Actors: Two to four elevator riders

6.10D

Situation: Lost in translation

Conflict: Two people are acting out a scene in an unknown language. Two other people are playing the voices of the translators.

Spice It Up: The director calls out different types of styles: soap opera, drama, western, horror, etc. Both the actors and their interpreters must continue the scene in the new style.

Themes: Perception, differences, communication, change, stereotypes

Actors: Two foreign actors and two translators

6.10E

Situation: Hey, the way I feel can be described best in a song!

Conflict: Pick any conflict from another section—friendship, dating, faith, etc.—and make the conflict a musical number. The actors break out into song according to what their characters and conflicts are all about.

Themes: Dependent on the conflict chosen

Actors: Dependent on the conflict chosen

6.10F

Situation: What does a person have to do to get a little bit of that toilet paper?

Conflict: Two people are sitting in their own individual stalls in a public restroom. Actor 1 really needs toilet paper and realizes he has none. He talks to Actor 2 through the wall of the bathroom stall to try to convince Actor 2 to share some toilet paper.

Themes: Crisis, vulnerability, sharing (greed), compassion, persuasion, embarrassment

Actors: Two actors

6.10G

Situation: Have you ever tried the fried spam?

Conflict: Two people at a restaurant place an order, each choosing what they consider to be the most delicious dish—though their choice is actually the worst, most disgusting thing imaginable to the other person. The server gets their orders mixed up, and the diners start to chow down on the food they've been given.

Themes: Differences, mistakes, misunderstanding, awkward situations

Actors: Two restaurant patrons and one server

6.10H

Situation: How does he do that?

Conflict: Modern-day professor has made a time machine in which he travels back to different periods of history (e.g., Prehistoric, Renaissance, Ice Age, Civil War, etc.). On his trips, the professor tries to talk to the people of that era.

Themes: Values, cultures, words, communication, change

Actors: One professor and four or five actors playing characters from the different eras

6.10I

Situation: Number four, please step forward.

Conflict: Four people are in a police lineup. A police officer helps a victim pick out the person who is responsible for the crime against her. Though the perpetrator couldn't be more obvious, the victim struggles to choose the right person.

Spice It Up: Use audience members for your lineup.

Themes: Focus, risk, judgment, differences, choices

Actors: Four actors for the lineup, one police officer, and one victim

6.10J

Situation: We don't have a clip, but if we did…

Conflict: One or two people portray news anchors, while a small group of three or four actors plays the members of a news crew. As the anchor introduces various topics of the news for that day, the news crew must act out "video clips" of whatever stories the anchor is conveying.

Spice It Up: If you want to use this with a lesson, give your anchor story ideas that go along with your message.

Themes: (Dependent upon topic chosen)

Actors: One or two news anchors and three or four news crew members

6.10K

Situation: Mom, Dad…you are such a geek.

Conflict: Daughter gets ready for the prom. Daughter loves her parents, but they sometimes look and act like the biggest geeks in the world. Mom and Dad cannot help but give safety advice and even demonstrate some dance moves for their daughter as she waits for her date.

Spice it Up: Daughter's date for prom rings doorbell; her parents want to "meet and greet."

Themes: Dating, parents, family, wisdom, respect

Actors: One mom, one dad, and one daughter (*Spice It Up:* One additional guy as date)

6.10L

Situation: The terrible twos

Conflict: Bible study teacher tries to get his young adult class to listen and participate in the class activity, but for some reason, they're all acting like absolute children.

Spice it up: Try different character traits from section 7.2.

Themes: Growing up, maturity, self-control, perseverance, patience

Actors: One teacher and four or five actors acting out different character traits

SCENARIOS

Here are the "nuts and bolts" you'll need to put together "meeeeellions" of improvs. Okay, maybe not millions, but at least hundreds. This "Scenarios" section contains bits and pieces of improv ideas that can be used to accentuate, build on, and even invent improvs. We've broken up the scenarios into five different categories to make this chapter easier for you to use. Here is an explanation of those categories:

SETTINGS

Every improv needs a point of origin, so we've listed 100 different locations where your characters can make things happen. From realistic to crazy, you'll find some great settings for your improvs.

CHARACTERS

You can only steal characters from Saturday Night Live for so long—and let's face it, some of those aren't so great anyway. So we've compiled 100 different types of characters for your improvs. Allow your actors to pick and choose who they want to be, or assign them a creative character to play.

OCCUPATIONS

Though sometimes it's helpful to choose a character specifically based on the type of job, these can be used as an extension of the "Characters" list in most improv games, significantly increasing the number of combinations your actors can create.

TRAITS

Everyone has those different little quirks that make them unique (some more so than others), and we've listed 100 different character traits to help bring your improv characters to life. Choose one for a character, or mix and match them to create truly outrageous (and confused!) characters.

FEELINGS

You probably didn't even know there were 100 different ways you could describe how you feel, did you? Well, now you do.

PROPS

If you use your imagination, one prop can easily be 10 different things. So, if you use your imagination, we've provided 1,000 different props for you. (Do that math...100 props we provided, times 10 different ways you can imagine using them, equals 1,000 props. We included this equation so the book can also be used in algebra classes!)

ACTIONS

A simple action would be walking. A more complex action would be juggling knives while driving a school bus filled with monkeys across an old narrow bridge. We've given you 50 of each kind. Have fun, and please take care of the monkeys.

LINES TO GET YOU GOING

No more staring at the ceiling trying to come up with an opening line. We have 100 lines here to get things rolling. Please note that we have provided some ideas for you in parentheses, but let that just be a starting point for you. Try to be as creative as you can be in coming up with your own ideas; that's what will make your improvs your own.

You can either let everyone involved know how you're going to start things, or you can give the clue to just one actor. Either way, these can kick things off and lead the scene in a multitude of different directions.

LINES TO END WITH

There aren't many things worse than an improv that just won't end. (Academy Award acceptance speeches, anybody?) So we put together 100 different closing lines to help you "shut her down"! Either that, or you can keep a pit orchestra ready to fire up that closing music—your choice.

Have your actors end with these lines to draw their improvisations to a close. You may want to assign the line to one of the actors before the situation starts or leave it open for your actors to determine which character would use it best. Just as with the "Lines to Get You Going," feel free to broadcast your wrap-up to the group, or keep it a secret until it comes out.

"Scenarios" are meant to be used either individually or grouped together to give your group some tools to work with in their skits. No doubt, you will find yourself coming back to this section again and again. Mathematically, can you imagine how many combinations of characters, traits, places, lines, and actors you and your group have the opportunity to toss together? You could literally have a brand new scene every time.

We hope you enjoy using these lists, along with the rest of this book, in your ministry as much as we have (and continue to) in ours. Thanks for all you do with young people, and thanks for giving us the opportunity to partner in ministry with you.

— EDDIE JAMES & TOMMY WOODARD (THE SKIT GUYS)

7.1 SETTINGS

1. Waiting in line
2. Movie theater
3. Tollbooth
4. Coffee shop
5. Preschool room
6. Waiting room
7. Principal's office
8. Emergency Room
9. Retirement home
10. Funeral
11. Elevator
12. Restaurant
13. Police lineup
14. Classroom
15. Guided tour
16. Rave
17. New Year's Eve in New York City
18. Dog park
19. Clothing store
20. Floor of the New York Stock Exchange
21. Hollywood movie set
22. Library
23. Religious service
24. Unstable coal mine
25. Community college
26. Drama rehearsal
27. Ballet
28. Concert
29. Building on fire
30. Scene of an arrest
31. Twelve-step group meeting
32. Television show from the 1950s
33. Restroom
34. Academy Awards show
35. Dark alley
36. Fourth of July parade
37. Popular talk show
38. Family vacation
39. Fishing trip
40. Hair salon
41. Fashion show
42. Local news station
43. Morgue
44. Hottest day of summer
45. Coldest day of winter

46. High school hallway

47. Camp

48. Small apartment

49. Group date

50. Assembly line

51. Dance

52. Locker room

53. Heaven

54. Hell

55. Inside someone else's brain

56. Convertible in a carwash

57. Zoo

58. Doctor's office

59. Airplane

60. Roller coaster

61. Deserted island

62. Time machine

63. Party

64. Bank

65. Courtroom

66. NASCAR race

67. Oval Office

68. Giant maze

69. Water treatment plant

70. Frozen lake

71. Desert

72. Prison

73. Space station

74. Trunk of a car

75. Square dance

76. Radio show

77. Dating service

78. Ballgame

79. Choir practice

80. Congress

81. Stairwell

82. Gas station

83. Mall

84. Parking lot

85. Mountaintop

86. U.S. Embassy in foreign country

87. Ski lift

88. Amusement park

89. Home kitchen

90. Very tall building

91. Museum

92. Bowling alley

93. Book store

94. College dormitory

95. Assembly line

96. Recording studio

97. Teachers' lounge

98. Hotel

99. Department store

100. Church sanctuary

For an added dimension, feel free to combine any two settings.

7.2 CHARACTERS

1. Redneck
2. Native American
3. Cowboy
4. Alien
5. Class clown
6. Grandparent
7. Mr./Miss Positive
8. The "whiner"
9. Cheerleader
10. Drunk person
11. Science geek
12. Middle school student with braces
13. Drama queen
14. The worst actor ever
15. Comic book character
16. Valley girl/surfer dude
17. Your pastor
18. Cartoon character
19. Hippie
20. Kindergartener
21. Mad scientist
22. Card shark
23. Pilot on his/her first day
24. Multimillionaire
25. Really bad psychologist/psychiatrist
26. Miss America (just been crowned)
27. Overbearing dad
28. Overprotective mom
29. Pesky younger sibling
30. Ex-boyfriend/ex-girlfriend
31. Skydiver
32. Infant or toddler
33. The ghost of someone who used to live here
34. The worst comedian ever
35. Test-car dummy
36. The tooth fairy
37. The president of a third-world country no one's ever heard of
38. Any biblical character
39. Prison inmate
40. Prison warden
41. Yoda
42. Barney
43. Satan

44. Monk/nun

45. Author on a book tour

46. Really bad public speaker

47. Spelling bee champion

48. Distant relative no one likes

49. Computer hacker

50. Genie

51. Angel

52. Demon

53. Video game champion of the world

54. Mob boss' accountant

55. Rain cloud hovering over a city

56. Olympic athlete in ancient Greece

57. Polo player

58. Racehorse

59. Any Monty Python character

60. Ballet dancer

61. The clumsiest person ever

62. Kid who desperately wants to be in the carnival

63. Chain smoker

64. Gang leader

65. Panhandler

66. Secretary who dislikes her boss

67. World champion hotdog eater

68. Retired professional athlete

69. Camp counselor

70. Really bad ventriloquist

71. Champion dodge ball player

72. Retired rock star

73. Geeky parent

74. Fake psychic

75. Hand model

76. Elephant poop scooper

77. Retired vice principal

78. Reality show contestant

79. Really bad magician

80. Stuntman who always gets hurt

81. Cast of *Seinfeld*

82. Leprechaun

83. Santa Claus

84. A person who is always sick

85. The most selfish person ever

86. Person with short-term memory loss

87. Samurai warrior

88. Compulsive movie watcher

89. Compulsive liar

90. The laziest person ever

91. Fast talker

92. Piano teacher from the '50s

93. The "mumbler"

94. A miserable clown

95. Real person suddenly transported into a TV character

96. Person turning 40 years old today

97. Person with irritable bowel syndrome

98. Billiard ball

99. Coffee pot

100. Any other inanimate object personified

7.3
OCCUPATIONS

1. Preacher
2. Fast-food worker
3. Forensic scientist
4. Stockbroker
5. Zookeeper
6. Insurance agent
7. Artist
8. Clown
9. Tightrope walker
10. Rock star
11. Internal Affairs officer
12. Stuntman/woman
13. Kid show entertainer
14. College professor
15. Obstetrician
16. Con artist
17. Model
18. Hockey player
19. Jockey
20. Drill sergeant
21. Football coach
22. Lion tamer
23. Farmer
24. Rancher
25. Computer technician
26. News anchor or weather person
27. Private detective
28. Used car salesperson
29. DJ or radio announcer
30. Tour guide
31. Self-help guru
32. Train engineer
33. King/queen
34. CIA agent
35. Kindergarten teacher
36. Cafeteria worker in a high school
37. Televangelist
38. Mime
39. Salesman
40. Rap artist
41. Carnival worker
42. Inventor
43. Mayor
44. Butler
45. Flight attendant
46. Pirate

47. Owner of a multinational corporation

48. Person with the most boring job in the world

49. Motivational speaker

50. Game show host

51. Waiter/waitress

52. Butler

53. Gas station attendant

54. Computer programmer

55. Traffic cop

56. Fisherman

57. Movie scriptwriter

58. Bodyguard for the President

59. Chef

60. Janitor

61. Drug dealer

62. United Nations ambassador

63. Newspaper deliverer

64. Camp counselor

65. Heavyweight boxer

66. Scuba diving instructor

67. Bartender

68. Door-to-door salesperson

69. Movie director

70. WWF wrestler

71. Firefighter

72. New York stage actor

73. Psychologist/psychiatrist

74. Surgeon

75. IRS agent

76. College student (who's been there for 10 years)

77. Political analyst

78. Hardware store clerk

79. Street sweeper

80. Electrician

81. Full-time parent

82. Unemployed

83. Figure skater

84. Youth minister (We hope you have a thick skin for this one)

85. Game warden

86. Auto mechanic

87. The voice behind most of America's infomercials

88. Dentist/orthodontist

89. U.S. senator

90. Sailor

91. Child movie star

92. Infantry soldier

93. Country music star (or wannabe)

94. Opera star

95. Shepherd

96. Prison guard

97. Judge

98. Attorney

99. NASCAR driver

100. Astronaut

7.4
TRAITS

1. Has a speech impediment (stutter, lisp, etc.)
2. Can't get rid of the hiccups
3. Has a twitch
4. Easily distracted
5. Has a cold/cough
6. Is fixated on everyone else's hair
7. Walks with a limp
8. Can't stop dancing
9. Gestures in an overly animated way
10. Has trouble controlling the volume of his voice
11. Keeps talking while eating
12. Can't stop smiling/crying
13. Is easily embarrassed
14. Flirts with someone in the crowd
15. Can't control gas
16. Cranky
17. Keeps clearing throat
18. Clumsy
19. Can't stop sneezing
20. Occasionally picks nose

21. Speaks and moves like a robot
22. Mimics everyone else
23. Has an itchy rash
24. Is paranoid
25. Starts almost every sentence with, "Now listen to me..."
26. Has the giggles
27. Speaks in movie/song titles
28. Can't stop mothering everyone
29. Bites fingernails
30. Speaks in a monotone voice
31. Sarcastic
32. Overly macho/feminine
33. Spells words thinking others won't know what's being said
34. Snaps and points finger at people for no reason
35. Ends almost every sentence with, "You know what I'm talkin' 'bout?"
36. Turns the focus of every conversation back to himself
37. Thinks she is a movie star
38. Thinks he is on a reality television show

39. Says "Yes!" in strange places in the conversation

40. Finds the negative element in everything

41. Talks to people like they are babies

42. Speaks only in clichés

43. Tries to diagnose everyone with a particular disorder

44. Periodically breaks out into song

45. Fast talker

46. Overly dramatic about nothing

47. Forgetful

48. Uses big words that don't fit or make sense in order to appear intelligent

49. Speaks with a distinct accent

50. Person with an imaginary friend (or other personality)

51. Gives one-word answers

52. Uses sound effects in place of certain words

53. Unable to stop touching others

54. Speaks only in rhyming couplets

55. Thinks he is a superhero

56. Can't hear very well

57. Repeats everything everyone else says

58. Gets too close physically (in others' personal space)

59. Constantly fidgets

60. Is afraid of germs

61. Can't make up her mind

62. Finishes everyone else's sentences

63. Always optimistic

64. Questions everything

65. Hears voices

66. Spits when talking

67. Likes to gossip

68. Easily angered

69. Insecure

70. Speaks some strange language no one else understands

71. Periodically falls asleep

72. Paralyzed from the waist down

73. Shy/reserved

74. Moves in slow motion

75. Hypochondriac

76. Stuck in the '60s

77. Stuck in the '70s

78. Stuck in the '80s

79. Has a broken limb

80. Ends every conversation with, "…and that's all I have to say about that."

81. Tries to correct everyone else

82. Walks backward

83. Whines about everything

84. Overly optimistic

85. Can't stop singing

86. Doesn't believe what anyone says

87. Can't speak

88. Begins every statement with, "Oh, I don't think so…"

89. Smacks own forehead every few seconds

90. Anytime someone touches him, responds with, "Thanks, I needed that."

91. Always having to "one-up" the others by being better, faster, more courageous, etc., and tell a story to back it up

92. Gets flashbacks to being on a deserted island for three years

93. Can't drink enough water to quench thirst

94. Every few minutes, thinks gravity is reversing

95. Any time someone says "the," puts hands over ears and screams in pain

96. Thinks everyone else is "Mom"

97. Believes all men are really Santa Claus

98. Constantly practicing "quick draw" gunslinger motion

99. Heckles everyone else as if they're all bad comedians

100. Falling more in love every moment

1. Sad
2. Obnoxious
3. Slow
4. Exhausted
5. Happy
6. Self-conscious
7. Terrified
8. Fearless
9. Confident
10. Cool
11. Arrogant
12. Confused
13. Giddy
14. Agitated
15. Disoriented
16. Concerned
17. Defiant
18. Defiled
19. Disgusted
20. Confused
21. Optimistic
22. Pessimistic
23. Nauseated
24. Funny
25. Shaky
26. Nervous
27. Bored
28. Thrilled
29. Choked up
30. Ecstatic
31. Embarrassed
32. Exasperated
33. Annoyed
34. Distracted
35. Ticked off
36. Jolly
37. Intrigued
38. Playful
39. Used
40. Dumb
41. Strong
42. Ambitious
43. Productive
44. Fat
45. Ugly
46. Insignificant

47. Paralyzed
48. Defensive
49. Melancholy
50. Worried
51. Disrespected
52. Depressed
53. Crushed
54. High
55. Hungry
56. Thirsty
57. Warm
58. Betrayed
59. Curious
60. Scared
61. Moody
62. Doubtful
63. Angry
64. Dull
65. Sullen
66. Injured
67. Carefree
68. Hurt
69. Belligerent
70. Bitter
71. Itchy
72. Nosey
73. Left out
74. Let down
75. Put down
76. Taken advantage of
77. Empty

78. Enthusiastic
79. Numb
80. Paranoid
81. Overly dramatic
82. Lonely
83. Tired
84. Flat
85. Hyper
86. Blissful
87. Distracted
88. Uptight
89. Sick
90. Calm
91. Unappreciated
92. Unimportant
93. Awed
94. Lonely
95. Nervous
96. Restless
97. Disappointed
98. Ashamed
99. Thankful
100. Lost

7.6
PROPS

1. Cowboy hat
2. Phone
3. Lamp
4. Bow and arrow
5. Big bowls
6. Basketballs/soccer balls
7. Picture frames
8. Computer keyboards
9. Paper sacks
10. Garbage cans
11. Crayons
12. Fake plants
13. Speaker pulpits
14. Hymnal
15. Microphone stand
16. Bag of potato chips
17. Ream of paper
18. Orange parking cones
19. Tithe envelopes
20. Bucket full of ice
21. Backpack
22. Choir robe
23. Big water gun

24. Video camera
25. Any old Christian music CDs
26. Leaf blower
27. Hammer
28. Gallon of milk
29. Pair of XXXL shorts or shirt
30. Toothpaste
31. Magazines
32. Hula skirt
33. Disco ball
34. Clothespins
35. Pillows
36. Soda cans
37. Briefcase
38. Baby bottle
39. Beanie with propeller
40. Mickey Mouse ears
41. Golf clubs
42. Wiffle ball bat
43. Different shaped balloons
44. Paintbrushes
45. Old wrapping paper tubes
46. Binoculars

47. Steering wheel
48. Bandanas
49. Wigs
50. Tennis rackets
51. Clown shoes
52. Big '70s sunglasses
53. Old band instruments
54. Books
55. Giant family Bible
56. Towels
57. Notebooks
58. Suitcases
59. Small TV
60. Old handheld video games
61. Old cell phones
62. Mirror
63. Hardhat
64. CD player and headphones
65. Extension cord
66. Pair of shorts
67. Curling iron
68. Candles
69. Sofa
70. Dinner table and chairs
71. Printer
72. Old black and white photos
73. Action figures
74. Confetti
75. Spaghetti noodles (dry)
76. Ice cream scooper
77. Tub of butter

78. Comics section of newspaper
79. Different sized baskets
80. Nerd glasses
81. Chunk of cheese
82. Different buckets
83. Feather boa
84. Winter coat
85. Chair
86. Weed trimmer
87. Inflatable swimming pool
88. Barbeque utensils
89. Lunch/dinner platter
90. Blow-up animals for pool
91. Old person glasses
92. Tie
93. Pile of pennies
94. Coat hanger
95. Scarf
96. Ping Pong paddles
97. Styrofoam cup
98. Pen
99. Swimming arm-floaties
100. Soup ladle

7.7A SIMPLE ACTIONS

1. Jumping jacks
2. Loves to smell clothes
3. Likes to look "longingly" into anyone's eyes
4. Checks armpits constantly
5. Scratches
6. Hops like a frog
7. Gallops like a horse
8. Becoming invisible
9. Can't stop dancing
10. Life of the party
11. Can't stop preaching
12. Auctioning
13. Drumming
14. Fighting
15. Working out
16. Ballet Dancing
17. Running
18. Doing mime
19. Riding a horse
20. Driving a car
21. Skipping
22. Scratching constantly

23. Stretching
24. Painting
25. Juggling
26. Trying to make a cell phone call with a bad signal
27. Sleeping
28. Sneaking around
29. Cooking
30. Building something
31. Always tying people's shoes
32. Bowling
33. Playing golf
34. Practicing karate moves
35. Doing yoga
36. Eating a meal
37. Trying to wake up a foot that's fallen asleep
38. Making "toot" noises with arm pit
39. Constantly rubbing eyes
40. Constantly picking nose
41. Constantly cleaning ears
42. Constantly fixing hair

43. Constantly making snorting sounds at the back of the throat

44. Constantly smelling fingertips

45. Building a house

46. Making a banana split

47. Watching a movie (Try different genres: comedy, drama, horror, etc.)

48. Washing a car

49. Cleaning a garage

50. Changing a flat tire

7.7B SLIGHTLY MORE COMPLEX ACTIONS

51. Always typing even when there is no computer

52. Constantly dancing to his own beat, which no one else hears

53. Voice goes up to a yell and then back down to a whisper in casual conversation

54. Thinks she is always in a musical and breaks out into song regularly

55. Starts every sentence off with, "I wish," then begins to demonstrate that wish, thinking everyone is too clueless to understand just by words

56. Trading stocks on the floor of the New York Stock Exchange

57. Army instructor with new recruits reporting for basic training

58. Scene in an elevator where each character is acting out a really disgusting habit or trait

59. Breaks out into monkey-like mannerisms to show feelings

60. Family eating spaghetti and meatballs

61. Students walking in a high school graduation ceremony

62. Rock group singing a sappy love ballad

63. Group of kids playing a popular video game

64. Party where there's drinking and one student refuses to drink

65. Dog trainers trying to get their dogs to listen

66. Group wanting to go swimming in a freezing lake

67. Bad magician doing tricks on a crowded corner

68. Couple getting married

69. Riding in a subway, each actor portraying different characters getting off at various times

70. Scientists working with nuclear waste

71. Astronauts who land on the moon and decide to play golf

72. Residents of a retirement home playing bingo

73. The making of a family portrait where everyone is not getting along

74. School dance where every person wishes he or she were with someone else, so they're trying to get with those people

75. Student being attracted to tutor while in the middle of a lesson

76. Bored students in a classroom with a dull teacher

77. Guy and girl watching a movie; guy tries to put moves on girl, but girl doesn't want anything to do with him

78. Firefighters putting out a fire

79. Two people arguing over one person's alleged bad breath; bad breath person is defensive; others in proximity smelling bad breath throughout

80. Emergency Room doctors and interns working on a patient

81. Cheerleaders doing a cheer

82. Playing hopscotch or double-Dutch jump rope

83. Hanging wallpaper

84. Kids playing in a moonwalk/bouncy house

85. Watching a sport (like tennis or Ping Pong)

86. Playing charades and doing a horrible job miming something that should be very easy to demonstrate

87. Jumping out of a plane with a parachute

88. Hiking up a mountain

89. Trying to mount a horse

90. Practicing a dance routine

91. Police officer directing traffic

92. Doing a speech in super-fast motion

93. Washing a car as if he had the slow-motion button on himself

94. Beginning to cry while watching a "chick flick"

95. Shooting a film and one actor cannot remember her line

96. Doing a gymnastics floor routine

97. Shooting a game of pool and losing horribly

98. Taking a flying lesson

99. Student taking his driver's test for the first time

100. Needing to go to the bathroom during a packed blockbuster movie and she is in the middle of a row

7.8
LINES TO GET YOU GOING

1. Where are we?

2. Can we talk about our fight yesterday?

3. Why do you keep avoiding me?

4. What took you so long?

5. Can I ask you something I've wanted to ask you for a long time?

6. Let me tell you how it all started…

7. Once upon a time…

8. So, what would happen if I asked you out again?

9. Your nose is bleeding!

10. Are you trying to make me hate you?

11. So, is what they say about _____ really true?

12. Is it just me, or is it you?

13. I couldn't help but notice you were… (juggling, sad, confused, etc.)

14. It's free?

15. How about that! She didn't even… (flinch, give me the time of day, say anything, etc.)

16. My arm has been hurting all day! It must have been that bizarre tractor accident.

17. Do you think he/she/it ever had a chance?

18. Whom were you talking with on the phone when I came in?

19. Why is it so hard for you to forgive me?

20. If you really knew me as well as you say you do, how could you accuse me of such a thing?

21. I'm struggling with something you said.

22. You want to know what I did to get that detention?

23. Why is your dad the way he is?

24. I hate to tell you this, but…

25. Did someone just pass gas?

26. Why is everyone looking at me?

27. So, is the rumor about you two true?

28. How do you feel about this whole crazy situation?

29. I heard what happened to your dog.

30. Now that's got to be the ugliest thing I've ever seen!

31. Holy Popsicle Sticks, Batman! What are we going to do?

32. Why is it every time you walk by me, you… (pass gas, start to laugh, roll your eyes, etc.)

33. I don't mean to be rude, but your _____ is in my turkey pot pie.

34. God has given me a vision, and I want to tell you about it!

35. Hey, my sister thinks you are… (hot, shy, mad at her, rude, etc.)

36. Look me in the eye and tell me the truth. I'm tired of your lies!

37. I cannot believe you just said that to me!

38. How do you like that—I finally get the nerve to tell her what I'm feeling, and wham!

39. Did you see me on TV yesterday?

40. Do my feet stink?

41. Mamma always said, "Life is like a _____" (can't say "box of chocolates").

42. You know, you're not fooling anybody here.

43. What was that sound?

44. I'm not trying to call you a liar, but…

45. I'm sorry, you're not allowed in here.

46. Well, somebody better come up with an idea fast!

47. Do you think this makes me look fat?

48. Holy Cow! What have you been eating?

49. Is it supposed to make that sound?

50. Umm…how do I say this?

51. A simple "thank you" sure would be nice right about now.

52. This is not what I ordered.

53. My parents said I can't date you anymore.

54. You look familiar. Have we met somewhere before?

55. Have you ever thought about this before?

56. Stop! Everyone, just stop it right now!

57. How *could* you?

58. Okay, which one of you is the owner of that savage Chihuahua?

59. I've just been informed that we're going to be here a lot longer than we originally planned.

60. We're trapped!

61. Okay, nobody move! We're getting to the bottom of this right now!

62. Don't look at me—I didn't do it!

63. So, you all decided to get together without me. That's just great! Well, I'm here...Now what?

64. Hey Doc, I'm getting this shooting pain right here every time I…

65. All right, I want some answers, and I want them now.

66. I'm not sure what that is (pointing at something). What do you think?

67. Well, if you all feel so strongly about it, then you do it.

68. Why do I always have to be the one who sticks up for you?

69. Are you sure this is legal?

70. Excuse me, did you say "suicide mission"?

71. Okay, everyone's name is in the hat (pretends to draw name). Sorry, _____, it looks like you're first.

72. I've got a bad feeling about this.

73. Have you ever asked yourself why we're doing this?

74. If Superman and Batman got into a fight, who do you think would win?

75. Hi...I'm your blind date.

76. I can't stand this anymore! Somebody do something!

77. Okay...okay, I'll do it. Just tell me how to do it...one more time.

78. Okay, who called this meeting?

79. I'm sorry, but is that your real hair?

80. Let's face it. We don't have a chance here.

81. I'm not saying we should break up; I'm just saying...

82. Help me, Doc! I keep having this dream where I become the ruler of the spaghetti kingdom and must defend all the little pasta people...What does it mean?

83. I need two volunteers to stay here. The rest will go with me.

84. If you love me, you'll do it. (Cannot be sexual in any way.)

85. Excuse me. Is this the bus to Nowhere?

86. He's dead.

87. They did it! I can't believe it— they actually did it!

88. Jack wanted me to tell you all he's sorry he couldn't be here. It seems he had to... (rescue a dolphin, talk to the president, go fly fishing with his uncle Julio, etc.)

89. I don't know about you losers, but I'm outta here!

90. Apparently, I forgot the keys, so what do we do now?

91. Duck!

92. Wait a minute...is this where you tell me I'm going to some boot camp for troubled kids?

93. I'm sorry, I couldn't hear you. Would you mind repeating that?

94. Am I crazy, or did that guy just flip me off?

95. Are you seeing/hearing/thinking what I'm seeing/hearing/thinking?

96. Poke it and see if it moves.

97. Would you mind looking at this rash?

98. Want to see my scar?

99. I can stick my whole fist in my mouth...Want to see?

100. Welcome to the second annual People Against Meetings meeting. Who would like to start?

LINES TO END WITH

1. So, this is how we end all this, huh?

2. I cannot believe you didn't even give me the benefit of the doubt.

3. I have no regrets. You?

4. So, whaddaya say, hot stuff?

5. Will I see you next week under the yellow umbrella?

6. Well, I can see this conversation has been useless.

7. I don't care what you say…not me. No way. Never again.

8. I gotta write that down.

9. What can I do for you?

10. *Now* what?

11. The sun sure did shine bright today.

12. All right, but *I'm* not going to be there.

13. I'll never forget you.

14. You are my hero.

15. I still think it should have been blue.

16. Later.

17. Don't forget what we had, okay?

18. What a day this has turned out to be.

19. As far as you know.

20. Do you really mean that?

21. Show me the money!

22. I can't believe you really thought I liked you!

23. Looks like rain again…looks like rain. Not that I'm a meteorologist or anything.

24. I thought this was going to be relaxing, but I totally underestimated you!

25. So, you weren't at the party after all?

26. I want my mommy!

27. I'm not moving.

28. What did you think was ever going to come of this anyway?

29. I love you, Dad.

30. See, the deal is…I kind of like you.

31. I want cookies!

32. Wow! Oh wow! Ummm… wow! I can't believe it this is happening to me! Wow!

33. By the way, you are really cute.

34. Save it, we're done.

35. I was just starting to believe you.

36. You were supposed to be my best friend.

37. You are a big reason I am the person I am today.

38. Don't let go!

39. Great! We're lost.

40. Thank goodness you got that booger out of your nose!

41. Do you think we'll ever feel this way again?

42. I really thought we were going to make it.

43. Can I call you sometime?

44. Hey, Mom, it's me. Just wanted to say I'm sorry.

45. Once a liar, always a liar.

46. I don't know about you, but I'm freezing!

47. My mama always told me if I couldn't say anything nice, not to say anything at all.

48. You self-centered creep!

49. I couldn't have said it any better.

50. I don't care who hears me, I'll shout it from the rooftops—I LOVE YOU!

51. Who wants waffles?

52. That still doesn't take away the fact you broke my _____.

53. If you happen to see me sometime, like on a crowded street somewhere, walk past me. Don't stop to say hello…just keep on going.

54. Do you want a cab?

55. Well…adios.

56. Just as I thought, you'll never change.

57. Just goes to show you, you can never have enough cherry Kool-aid.

58. I'll think about it.

59. God, am I supposed to feel this way?

60. God, I don't know how much I can take—please do something… anything.

61. I'm so scared. Please help me.

62. You never did like my _____, did you?

63. Until we meet again…

64. You want fries with that?

65. Right now, it feels like I'll never get over this.

66. Save it for a rainy day, sister.

67. That's all, folks!

68. I'm outta here!

69. Well…um…thank you…I guess.

70. See, now that didn't hurt at all.

71. I'm still waiting.

72. I *mean* it this time.

73. Then I guess I'll have to say goodbye.

74. Sorry about that smell.

75. Oh…just forget it!

76. My dad was right about you.

77. There are no words for this—none that fit, anyway.

78. So then, I guess we'll have to finish this later.

79. Well, the next time I see you, I'll be the new spokesperson for… (Rolaids, banana bread, UNICEF, etc.)

80. I guess this wasn't really a date then, huh?

81. Next time I'll come more prepared…I promise.

82. Wow, I didn't see that one coming.

83. Wanna race?

84. I'm going to go get my dad.

85. Hey! You remembered!

86. See you in the funny papers, freak!

87. Well then, I guess I'll just limp away.

88. Uh…I think I just heard my mom calling. I've got to go.

89. Well, this sure was awkward!

90. Tell me something I don't know!

91. Then I guess I'll just get my stuff and go. Goodbye.

92. If you see her, tell her…tell her… oh, just forget the whole thing.

93. You act like that's a bad thing.

94. I'm sorry. I really am sorry, and I wish I could take it all back.

95. I'm leaving (starting to back away). I'm serious, I'm leaving (continuing to back away slowly). Look, I'm out the door. If you don't say something right now, I'll leave and never come back. (From offstage) I'm approaching the elevators. I'm getting in the elevator. I'm seriously going to leave. (Running back onstage) Are you really going to let it end this way? Because I thought you would have said something by now!

96. Well, that was five minutes of my life I can never get back.

97. If anyone needs me, I'll be in the can.

98. I'll have to come back later and clean that up.

99. I've got to go—_____ starts in 10 minutes.

100. Whatever!

THEME INDEX FOR "SCRIPTURE SKITS" AND "CHARACTER CONFLICTS"

Abandonment	(CC 6.2e)
Abortion	(CC 6.7l)
Abuse	(CC 6.7b, 6.7j)
Acceptance	(CC 6.2d, 6.5j, 6.6f, 6.7h, 6.10c)
Accountability	(CC 6.8c, 6.9a, 6.9e)
Actions (deeds)	(CC 6.4b, 6.8c, 6.9e, 6.9f)
Addiction	(CC 6.3d, 6.9a, 6.9e)
Adoption	(CC 6.2e)
Adversity (hardship)	(SS 3.5, CC 6.2a, 6.8j)
Ambition	(CC 6.5i, 6.5k)
Anger (rage)	(CC 6.2e, 6.2j, 6.3j, 6.5g, 6.6k, 6.7f)
Appearance	(SS 3.10, CC 6.1c)
Arguing	(SS 3.12, CC 6.1a)
Arrogance	(CC 6.4b, 6.5e)
Attitude	(CC 6.3c, 6.3i)
Awkward situations	(CC 6.1b, 6.1d, 6.1e, 6.10g)
Authenticity (real)	(CC 6.2d, 6.4i, 6.9c)
Authority	(SS 3.17, 3.19, CC 6.2f)
Belief (disbelief, atheism)	(SS 3.18, 3.20, 3.30, CC 6.4a, 6.4g, 6.4k, 6.8b, 6.8h, 6.9d)
Betrayal	(CC 6.6c)

Family	(CC 6.2c, 6.2l, 6.8g, 6.10a, 6.10k)
Fear (anxiety)	(SS 3.5, 3.29, CC 6.1b, 6.2b, 6.5h, 6.8d)
Feelings	(CC 6.1i, 6.1j, 6.3b)
Focus	(SS 3.21, 3.23, CC 6.3a, 6.10i)
Forgetfulness	(CC 6.5a, 6.5g)
Forgiveness (grace)	(SS 3.15, 3.17, 3.24, 3.25, 3.27, CC 6.4l, 6.6a, 6.6j, 6.6k, 6.8e, 6.8k)
Freedom	(CC 6.7j, 6.8e)
Friendship	(CC 6.1d, 6.4c, 6.4d, 6.4e, 6.4h, 6.5c, 6.6a, 6.6c, 6.6g, 6.6l, 6.7b)
Future	(CC 6.1j, 6.2b, 6.6i)
Generosity	(CC 6.6b)
Glory of God	(SS 3.17, 3.28, 3.30)
Goals	(CC 6.5k)
Gospel	(SS 3.18)
Gossip	(CC 6.1c, 6.5c, 6.6a)
Gratitude	(SS 3.16, 3.25)
Greed (sharing)	(CC 6.6b, 6.9j, 6.10f)
Grief (loss, sadness)	(SS 3.28, CC 6.3e, 6.3h, 6.8l)
Growing up	(CC 6.2g, 6.2i, 6.10l)
Habits	(CC 6.10c)
Hardship (adversity)	(SS 3.5, CC 6.8j)
Healing	(SS 3.16, 3.17, 3.25, 3.30, CC 6.7i, 6.7j)
Hearing (listening)	(CC 6.3a)
Hiding	(CC 6.7i)
Holiness (purity)	(CC 6.7c, 6.8e)
Homosexuality	(CC 6.7h)
Honesty (lying)	(SS 3.4, 3.8, CC 6.1d, 6.1e, 6.1g, 6.3i, 6.1j, 6.3k, 6.3l, 6.5b, 6.6c, 6.6j, 6.6k, 6.7b, 6.7c, 6.7e, 6.8e)
Hope	(CC 6.8d, 6.8g, 6.9i)
Humiliation	(CC 6.3f, 6.5j)

Humility	(CC 6.6k)
Hurt (pain)	(CC 6.1a, 6.6e, 6.7i, 6.7j, 6.8g)
Hypocrisy	(CC 6.4b, 6.7a)
Idols (idolatry)	(SS 3.26, CC 6.9h)
Image	(CC 6.3j, 6.7d, 6.7e, 6.9h)
Independence	(CC 6.2g, 6.2i)
Indulgence (excess)	(CC 6.9k)
Influence	(CC 6.2k, 6.4l, 6.5i, 6.6d, 6.7f, 6.9b, 6.10b)
Inner Worth (value)	(SS 3.10, CC 6.1b, 6.2e, 6.6f, 6.6g, 6.7d, 6.8e)
Innocence (guilt)	(CC 6.3a, 6.4l, 6.5d)
Integrity	(CC 6.1e, 6.3g, 6.3i, 6.5b, 6.9c)
Internet	(CC 6.7c, 6.9i)
Insecurity	(CC 6.1b)
Jealousy (envy)	(CC 6.3l, 6.6h, 6.9j)
Judgment	(CC 6.3a, 6.3b, 6.4c, 6.10i)
Justice	(SS 3.4)
Knowledge	(CC 6.7g, 6.8b, 6.9d)
Leadership	(CC 6.2k, 6.5a, 6.5i, 6.10b)
Legacy	(CC 6.2b, 6.5k)
Lifestyle	(CC 6.1l, 6.8c, 6.9f, 6.9g, 6.10a)
Listening (hearing)	(CC 6.3a, 6.6a)
Loneliness	(CC 6.3h, 6.6h, 6.7h)
Love	(SS 3.15, 3.22, 3.24, CC 6.1f, 6.1k, 6.2c, 6.3h, 6.4g)
Loyalty	(CC 6.6a, 6.6h)
Lust	(SS 3.8, CC 6.1c)
Malice (spite)	(CC 6.2j, 6.6e, 6.7a)
Marriage	(CC 6.7l)
Maturity	(CC 6.2g, 6.5k, 6.6i, 6.10l)
Materialism	(SS 3.26, 3.27, CC 6.6h, 6.9j)
Memories	(CC 6.2c, 6.4c, 6.6i)

Provision of God   (SS 3.3, 3.11, 3.20, CC 6.8d)

Purpose   (CC 6.3c, 6.4k, 6.9b)

Quality Time   (CC 6.3h)

Rationalization   (CC 6.3g, 6.9f, 6.9g)

Real (authenticity)   (CC 6.2d, 6.4i, 6.9c)

Rebellion   (CC 6.2f, 6.3d)

Redemption   (CC 6.4l, 6.8e)

Recognition   (CC 6.5e)

Regret   (CC 6.1l, 6.2j, 6.5l, 6.8e)

Rejection   (CC 6.4d, 6.4j, 6.5j, 6.6h)

Relationships   (CC 6.1a, 6.1d, 6.1f, 6.1i, 6.1k, 6.2c, 6.2e, 6.6i, 6.6j)

Religions   (CC 6.8b, 6.9d)

Reputation   (SS 3.27)

Rescue   (SS 3.7)

Respect   (SS 3.13, 3.14, CC 6.1c, 6.2f, 6.2h, 6.2l, 6.5e, 6.10k)

Responsibility   (SS 3.29, CC 6.1f, 6.2b, 6.2g, 6.3f, 6.3i, 6.3k, 6.4f, 6.5g, 6.9e, 6.9l)

Risk   (CC 6.6l, 6.9i, 6.10i)

Routine   (CC 6.8a)

Rumors   (CC 6.5c)

Sacrifice   (SS 3.26, CC 6.3h)

Safety   (CC 6.3f)

Salvation   (SS 3.15, CC 6.4d)

Searching   (CC 6.4k, 6.8a, 6.8b)

Secrets   (CC 6.6c, 6.7b, 6.7e, 6.9e)

Self-control   (CC 6.9k, 6.10l)

Self-esteem   (CC 6.3b, 6.6f, 6.7e)

Selfishness (unselfishness)   (SS 3.12, 3.23, 3.24, 3.26, CC 6.1g, 6.1k, 6.6h, 6.8i, 6.9h)

Self-mutilation   (CC 6.7i)

Hollywood would like to help you

Videos That Teach 2
RETAIL $12.99
ISBN 0-310-23818-8

Videos That Teach
RETAIL $12.99
ISBN 0-310-23115-9

Videos That Teach 3
RETAIL $12.99
ISBN 0-310-25107-9

Your students love movies, so why not utilize the movies they're watching to teach them valuable lessons. *Videos That Teach* products are for junior high, high school, college, and adult teachers and leaders. Each book contains 75 movie clip ideas from popular Hollywood films that illustrate a point or can be the point of an entire talk. *Videos That Teach* products are written by veteran youth workers Doug Fields and Eddie James and have been field tested by the authors.

visit www.youthspecialties.com/store
or your local Christian bookstore

Youth Specialties